Low Cost, No Cost Ideas for Youth Ministry

Group
Loveland, Colorado

Low Cost, No Cost Ideas for Youth Ministry
Copyright © 1994 Group Publishing, Inc.

Credits
Compiled and edited by Michael Warden and Mike Nappa
Interior designed by Lisa Smith
Interior illustrations by RoseAnne Buerge
Cover designed and illustrated by DeWain Stoll

Library of Congress Cataloging-in-Publication Data
Low cost, no cost ideas for youth ministry/compiled by the
    editors of Group Publishing.
        p. cm.
    ISBN 1-55945-187-4
    1.Church group work with teenagers. I. Group Publishing.
BV4447.L68 1994
259'.23--dc20   93-40019
                                                                      CIP

12 11 10 9 8 7 6 5 4 3   04 03 02 01 00 99 98 97 96 95

Printed in the United States of America.

Contents

Introduction 5

LOW COST, NO COST
Games 7
Low-prep activities that provide high levels of fun.

LOW COST, NO COST
Bible Studies and Devotions 25
Meaningful activities that carry a powerful point.

LOW COST, NO COST
Parties and Projects 47
Inexpensive celebration and service ideas.

LOW COST, NO COST
"Out of Bounds" Ideas 63
Ideas for youth groups away from church grounds.

LOW COST, NO COST
Holiday Ideas 81
Creative ways to observe special days throughout
the year.

LOW COST, NO COST
Food Ideas 97
Inexpensive ways to include food in youth ministry.

LOW COST, NO COST
**Outrageous Activities Using
Everyday Stuff** 111
Fun activities that use ordinary items in surprising
ways.

LOW COST, NO COST
Fund-Raisers 129
Quick ways to raise money without having to
invest a mint.

Contributors

Many thanks to the following people, who loaned us their creative expertise to bring together this volume of ideas:

David Adams
Mike Baer
Linda Barr
Michael Capps
David Cassady
Karen Ceckowski
Rick Chromey
Bryan Fink
Dick Hardel
Margie Hart
Lois Keffer
Paul Kelly
Lisa Lauffer
Scot Longyear
Christina Medina
Walter H. Mees Jr.
Amy L. W. Nappa
Pam Painter
Stephen Parolini
Skip Seibel
Bob Mio Sheldon
Steve and Annie Wamberg
Michael Warden
Paul Woods
Carol Younger

Introduction

Have you ever tried to run a first-class youth ministry on a fourth-class budget?

If you have, you're not alone. Many youth leaders struggle to stretch their budget dollars to impossible lengths.

Well, we've got good news for you. In response to the need for more cost-effective programming, the editors at Group Publishing have compiled this volume: *Low Cost, No Cost Ideas for Youth Ministry*.

This book contains a veritable gold mine of ideas—over 120 in all. You can use these ideas right now with your youth group—and while they don't require a big budget, they still produce big-time results.

In the following sections, you'll find ideas for low cost games, Bible studies, devotions, parties—even fund-raisers. You'll discover inexpensive ways to take your group out on the town. You'll learn creative options for serving others without exhausting your bank account. You'll find inexpensive ideas for celebrating holidays and fun ways to feed large groups of people with little or no cost to the church. And you'll benefit from the cost-cutting tips sprinkled throughout the book—practical suggestions for day to day savings in your ministry.

Low Cost, No Cost Ideas for Youth Ministry is more than just a book—it's a tool to help you run a full-time ministry on a part-time budget.

So go ahead and turn the page. Take a look at what's inside. You'll like what you see.

LOW COST, NO COST
Games

Low-prep activities that provide
high levels of fun.

Teenagers don't need a reason to have fun, and you don't need a reason to help them have fun. What you *do* need are low-prep games that provide high levels of fun. What a coincidence! An entire chapter of low cost, no cost games devoted entirely to fun rests in your hands right now.
So what are you waiting for? Let the games begin!

Balloon Tick-Tack-Toe

Use masking tape to "draw" two tick-tack-toe boards on the floor that are about 15 feet apart. Tape an inflated balloon inside each square of the two boards. Create "darts" by securely taping two pushpins to the end of a pencil.

Form two teams—the X's and O's—and have teams line up single file about five feet away from their tick-tack-toe boards (see the diagram).

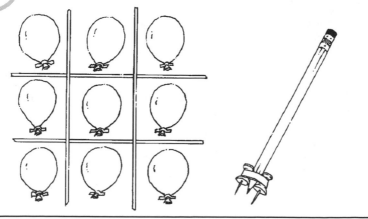

Give the first person in each line a dart. Have team members take turns tossing their darts at the balloons. The first team to pop three balloons in a row, either diagonally, across, or up and down, wins. Replace the popped balloons and play as many rounds as you want.

Note: Caution kids to handle the pushpin darts carefully and to never throw the darts (even jokingly) in a direction where a person might be hit. Also, over-inflating the balloons will cause them to pop more easily.

 Canned Races

use small water cups or Balloons

Designate a start and finish line for a race, then form pairs. Give each pair a freshly opened soft drink can and have partners stand back to back along the starting line with their soft drink can pressed between their shoulders.

Tell pairs the object of this game is to run to the finish line in the shortest amount of time without spilling their soft drinks. Begin the race. Award a prize to the pair that finishes first and a prize to the pair with the driest shirts at the end of the race.

Card-Castle Contests

Form teams of four. Give each team a pack of index cards and instruct team members to build a card castle within 10 minutes. The winning castle can be the highest one, the most creative design, or the strongest structure (test the structure using the

"I'll huff and I'll puff" method).

Once the basic structures are built, try these other card-building twists:

- Tell teams to add onto their castles without talking.
- Have teams build bridges to two other teams' castles.
- Declare a war. Give each team a stack of newspapers and 10 minutes to build a wall to protect its castle. Then have teams use paper wads to launch an attack on other castles from behind their own castle walls. The team whose castle is left standing after five minutes wins.

<table>
<tr><td>

COST-CUTTING TIP

Logo Splash—Shirts and other inexpensive items with your group's logo splashed all over are a fun way to identify members and foster a sense of belonging. Make sure the shirt's cost doesn't exclude anyone. Raise enough money to buy a shirt for everyone. And publicize how the shirts will be paid for so parents don't label the youth group as just another expense.

</td></tr>
</table>

 # Card Wars

Form two teams—team A and team B—and have teams stand facing each other at least five feet apart. Number two sets of 3×5 cards from one to 15 (one set for each team). Shuffle each set of 3×5 cards, then give each team member a card from his or her team's set. Tell kids not to show their cards to the other team.

Say: **The object of this game is to get everyone to join your team. You gain new team members by winning a 3×5 card "duel." A duel is played like this:**

- **One at a time, a representative from each team comes to the middle of the room to duel.**
- **For the first round, the representative from team A guesses whether he or she will win (have a higher number card), lose (have a lower card), or tie this duel.**

- **Next, both players in the duel display their cards. If the person from team A guessed right, both players join team A. If the person from team A guessed wrong, both players join team B.**
- **Then we'll repeat the duel with new players, but for the second round the representative from team B guesses the outcome. We'll continue alternating guessers each round.**

After everyone has dueled once, reshuffle the 3×5 cards and have kids continue play with new cards. Play until all kids are on one team, or until time expires.

Note: If your group has more than 30 students, you'll need to increase the number of cards in each team's set. Make sure you have at least one 3×5 card for each student.

Flying Sock Foot Race

Form two teams and have everyone remove his or her shoes and socks. Have each person tie his or her socks together and place them in a bowl (one bowl for each team). Make sure each team has an equal number of knotted socks. Then have team members lie on their backs side by side in a line.

Place each team's sock-filled bowl near the feet of the first person in each line. Place an empty bowl near the feet of the last person in each line (one bowl for each team).

Say: **Use your bare feet to pass**

the socks down your team's line and into the empty bowl. The first team to transfer all the socks wins. Ready? Go.

Maim That Tune

Before this game, arrange to have someone bring a musical instrument to class, such as a violin, guitar, or portable keyboard. You may also use a piano or church organ.

Ask kids to line up based on the number of years of music or voice lessons they've had (from most to least). You may have many or few kids with musical experience. Have kids count off by twos to form two teams that have approximately the same musical experience.

Say: **We're going to play a game called Maim That Tune. The object of the game is to quickly guess songs your teammates play on this** (instrument to be used). **Here's how the game works.**

Teams will take turns having a volunteer play a song on the instrument for his or her team to guess. The volunteer will choose the song to play but may not tell anyone what it is. I'll keep track of the time it takes to guess the songs, and we'll total the time for each team to determine the winner.

If you don't know how to play the instrument, just fake it. Remember, the rhythm is often just as memorable as the tune. You can choose any song you'd like to play as long as it's one that's been on the radio. As each person comes up to play a song, he or she must whisper the title to me before beginning. If your team can't guess the song within 30 seconds, the other team gets one guess. If that team guesses correctly, I'll subtract five seconds from its total time.

Play as many rounds as time allows, each time

having a different volunteer from each group attempt to play a song. Keep track of the total time from the first note played until the correct guess is made. Add up the total time it took to guess the songs. Declare the team with the lowest time the winners.

Newspaper Warriors

Give newspaper and masking tape to each teenager. Then allow about five minutes for teenagers to create newspaper swords and shields according to the diagram.

Roll and tape the newspaper to create six rods.

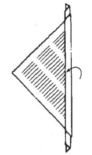

Roll one rod diagonally to make it longer than the others, and use it as your sword.

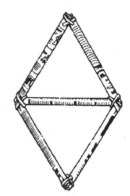

Securely tape together the other five rods in the shape shown in this diagram. That will provide the frame for the shield.

Cover one side of the shield's frame with a sheet of newspaper and securely tape the newspaper to the outer edge of the frame.

Now you have a shield to go along with your sword!

Tell everyone that the object of this game is to poke holes in other people's shields without allowing their own shields to be punctured. Group members can only use their swords to poke holes—nothing else allowed. Say "go" and let the free-for-all begin.

Call time every two minutes or so. Have kids whose shields have become "holey" move to one side. Then continue play until only one person is left with an intact shield. Declare this person the champion and award him or her a newspaper crown.

Note: Caution group members not to get too rough during this game. If your group is particularly boisterous, you might want to have guys play against guys and girls play against girls.

On-the-Wall Charades

Before the game, create a list of one- or two-syllable words. Clear a large space on the wall and form two teams. Have each team choose a representative to start the game.

Explain to kids that you'll show their selected team members a word that they must convey to their team. Tell kids they must convey the word in only one way: by using their heads as imaginary pencils to spell the words on the wall. Play several rounds so each team member gets a turn at writing on the wall. The team that's able to guess the correct answers in the shortest amount of time wins.

# Outdo Each Other

Use this game to help your teenagers experience the joy of serving others. Give group members each an "Outdo Each Other" handout (p. 17), a piece of masking tape, and a pencil. Instruct students to tape the handout onto each other's back.

Say: **We're going to have a service contest. Each of you has a list of services on your back that you need to have done for you. The idea is to outdo everyone else by doing the service items listed on their backs before all the items on your list are completed. When you do a service for someone else, sign the appropriate area on their handout. No one may refuse to be served, and you may only sign off a maximum of three items per list.**

If your list gets filled with names, move it to your front and continue to work at filling out others' lists. The last person with a list on his or her back is the winner. Ready? Go serve!

Spark discussion after the game by asking:

● **How would you describe the atmosphere in the classroom while you were all trying to outdo one another in serving?**

● **What would life be like if all Christians had an attitude about serving like the one that was needed to win this contest?**

Outdo Each Other

Try to do as many of the items below for others in the group before they do them all for you. Sign the space next to the items you do on each person's sheet.

- I have no hands. Will you comb my hair? _____
- I have no hands. Will you scratch my nose? _____
- I'm lost. Will you help me find my chair? _____
- I haven't learned how yet. Will you tie my shoes? _____
- I'm feeling a little sick. Will you draw me a map to the restroom? _____
- I'm color blind. Please help me find someone with red on. _____
- I'm shy. Will you help me find a date? _____
- I'm thirsty. Will you draw me a map to the water fountain? _____
- I forgot my Bible. Will you get me one I can use? _____
- I'm blind. Will you hold onto my arm for the rest of the game? _____
- I'm so scared. Will you hold my hand for the rest of the game? _____
- My hands are sore. Will you take my shoes off for me? _____
- I'm new. Will you introduce me to the teacher? _____
- I'm sad. Will you help me get hugs from two people? _____
- I can't reach it. Will you scratch my back? _____

Psychiatrist

Form a circle. Ask for two volunteers to play the "psychiatrists." Tell the psychiatrists that their job will be to work together to make an accurate diagnosis of the group's psychological problem. Then have the volunteers leave the room.

Once the pair is gone, have the remaining group members choose one of the following psychological problems to act out for the psychiatrists:

● **Kids each believe they're part of an elevator,** such as the doors, the pulleys, the bell, and the emergency stop button. Whenever the psychiatrist asks a question of any group member, he or she responds by making a door-opening sound, a bell sound, or whatever is appropriate for his or her elevator part.

● **Kids each believe they're the person sitting to their right.** They answer all questions as though they are that person. Just to make it more interesting, they each also have a fear of the word "but." Each time they hear it, the whole group panics and changes seats.

● **Kids each believe they're different characters from the show** *Star Trek: The Next Generation* (or another show popular with your youth group). Without giving their names, kids respond to all questions as though they are their assigned character. A variation could be kids believing that when they sit in particular chairs they become specific characters from the series. Then each time kids switch seats, their identities change.

After your group has chosen a psychological problem, call the psychiatrists back in the room. Allow the psychiatrists to ask any questions they like of any group member. Tell teenagers to answer all questions honestly without giving away the secret psychological problem. Any time a group member feels the psychiatrists are getting too close to the solution, he or she can yell out "psychiatrist," and have everyone move to a different place in the room.

Have kids come up with their own psychological problems and play several rounds, allowing various pairs to play the role of the psychiatrists.

Rush Hour

Beginning with one and ending with the total number of people in your group, have kids number off. Then have them arrange their chairs in two straight lines facing each other with an open space down the middle. Choose one person at random to become the "traffic cop," and have him or her stand between the lines of chairs. Remove the traffic cop's chair from the lines.

Tell the traffic cop to call out three or more numbers. The people with those numbers must exchange seats with each other. Tell the traffic cop that he or she must try to sit down as well. Whoever is left standing then becomes the new traffic cop. For added fun the traffic cop can randomly yell, "Rush hour!" and everyone has to try to exchange seats with the person sitting across from him or her while the traffic cop tries to sit down.

Soft Drink Babies

This game works great for a "guys night out" event. Form pairs and give each pair a baby bottle filled with a chilled soft drink, such as Coke or Pepsi. Have the youngest person in each pair be the "baby" and the older person be the "mother." Explain that pairs will race by having the mothers feed the babies the entire bottle of soft drink, then burp their babies by patting them on the back.

The first baby to burp after finishing the whole bottle wins.

 # Stunt Time

Here's a game you can use to spice up any youth meeting. You'll need two large pickle jars for this activity. Label one "Stunt Jar" and the other "People Jar."

On separate slips of paper write stunts that kids could perform at a moment's notice in your youth group meetings. For example, stunts might be "Perform a skit advertising an upcoming event," "Leapfrog the length of the room," "Sing the Taco Bell jingle," or "Make jungle noises." Write 20 stunts and place these slips of paper into the Stunt Jar.

For the People Jar, write categories describing kids in your group, such as "Everyone wearing red," "Everyone that lives within five miles of the church," or "Everyone wearing clothing with a team name on it." Create about 20 categories. Put these slips of paper into the People Jar.

During a youth meeting, call out: **Stunt time!** Then

pull a slip of paper out of each jar. Call the appropriate people to the front, then give them one minute to organize themselves and perform the stunt. Afterward, award prizes to those who performed during stunt time.

Tricky Toothpicks

Form two teams and give each team a box of toothpicks. Explain that on "go," each team will pass the box from person to person, only after each person spells his or her first name with the toothpicks. The only rule is that toothpicks may not be broken or bent in any way to form a letter. The first team to have its members each spell their name in toothpicks wins.

Up-in-the-Air Hockey

Form two teams. Give each person two balloons— one regular, round balloon and one long, narrow balloon. Have kids each blow up and tie off their balloons. Tell kids the round balloons serve as hockey pucks and the long balloons serve as hockey sticks.

Give teams a moment to brainstorm a team name, then have kids use markers to write their team name on their round balloons. At each end of the room, set up a large trash can as a goal.

Tell kids the object of this game is to get as many of their team's balloons into the other team's goal by hitting the round balloons with the long ones. Once a balloon is in a goal, the balloon can't be removed.

The first team to get all its balloons into the other team's trash can wins.

Very Important People, Places, and Things

Here's a fun mixer to help kids get to know more about the Bible. Before the meeting, write on separate 3×5 cards the names of famous biblical people, places, and things. For example, for famous people you might write "Samson," "Pontius Pilate," or "Simon Peter." A famous place could be the "Red Sea," "Bethlehem," or "Jesus' tomb." Famous things could be "manna," "Gideon's fleece," or "the cross."

As the kids arrive, tape a 3×5 card on each of their backs. Tell kids that these cards are their name tags, but they must figure out who or what they are. Tell group members to ask each other "yes" or "no" questions in order to figure out what's written on the cards.

For example, someone might ask, "Am I a person? A place? A thing?" "Did I build the ark?" or "Did I part the Red Sea for the Israelites to cross on dry land?" Be sure kids don't tell each other what the 3×5 cards say—they may only answer "yes" or "no." The game is over when everyone discovers what's written on his or her card.

What's My Phobia?

Compile a list of phony phobias for teenagers to act out. Include only phobias that can be easily acted out in the meeting room. For example, the list could include

- Smirkophobia (fear of people grinning)
- Sneakophobia (fear of tennis shoes)
- Songophobia (fear of singing people)
- Wastophobia (fear of paper trash)
- Earwaxophobia (fear of earwax)
- Jeanophobia (fear of denim)
- Hairophobia (fear of hair)

Have each team select a person to be its "phobic." Secretly assign the phobics the first fear on your list. Then tell the teams that they must each interact with their phobic until they uncover what his or her assigned phobia is. Explain that teams can interact with their phobics in any way they wish—but the phobics are not allowed to talk or point (although they can make noises). The first team to identify the phobia wins the round.

For each round, have teams select a new phobic. The team that identifies the most phobias wins.

LOW COST, NO COST
Bible Studies and Devotions

Meaningful activities that carry a powerful point.

Research indicates that teenagers learn best through active, involving experiences. But how can you provide meaningful, hands-on activities without spending an arm and a leg? Easy—use one of these Bible study or devotion ideas next time you want to teach a powerful truth in an innovative, yet inexpensive, way.

Affirmation Puzzle

Create a puzzle design on a sheet of paper. The design can be in the shape of a cross, a heart, or anything you wish. Draw dotted lines on your design to indicate where the puzzle pieces should be cut out. Make enough photocopies of the puzzle (on card stock paper) for each group member to have one.

Form a circle and give each person a copy of the puzzle and a pen. On their puzzles, have kids each write a note to the person seated three places to their right. The note should tell that person why the youth group wouldn't be complete without him or her. If necessary, remind group members to focus on positive things. For example, teenagers might write, "We wouldn't have your cheerfulness" or "We wouldn't have your caring attitude."

When kids finish, provide scissors and have them cut apart their puzzles. On the back of each puzzle piece have kids write the name of the person their note is for.

Combine all the puzzle pieces into one pile in the center of the circle and set out several rolls of cellophane tape. Tell kids their job is to search through the pile and use the tape to permanently reassemble puzzle notes meant for them.

When everyone is finished, have kids take turns reading aloud what's written on their puzzles. Then read aloud *Romans 12:4-16*. Ask:

● **How would our youth group be different if we refused to contribute something positive to it?**

● **As members of this group, how are we like pieces of a puzzle?**

● **How does it make you feel to hear the ways we all contribute to our youth group?**

Say: **Everyone in Christ's body is special: No one is expendable. You each belong here as a unique piece of the "puzzle" that makes up our youth group. Let's take a moment to thank God for the individual people in this group.**

Lead kids in a prayer of thanks, naming group members and thanking God for each one as you pray.

 # Body Drama

Form groups of four to six. On separate 3×5 cards, write different body parts, such as "hand," "eye," "ear," "mouth," "legs," or "nose." Give each group a different card and tell groups to prepare to act out what's on their cards for everyone else. Each person in a group must play a role in acting out the body part he or she has been assigned.

For example, one person can curl up to form the palm of a hand while others pretend to be fingers. Explain that the goal is to demonstrate the body part in such a convincing way that everyone else will easily guess what it is.

When groups are ready, have them take turns acting out their assigned body parts. Have nonperforming groups guess the body parts being acted out. Afterward congratulate kids for their ingenuity in the way they created hands, legs, eyes, or other body parts. Ask:

● **What made this activity easy or difficult for you?**

● **How did it feel to work together in this activity?**

● **What can we learn from this activity about how we should work together in service to Christ?**

Read aloud *1 Corinthians 12:12-27*. Then ask:

● **Why do you think God chose to compare the church to a body?**

● **What was the hardest thing about working together to create your body part?**

● **What's the hardest thing about working together as the body of Christ?**

● **How can we discover our roles in the body of Christ?**

● **What can we do as a youth group to become "one body" that's working together for Christ?**

Say: **Just as each of us had a role to play in the activity, each of us has a role to play in the body of Christ. This week, remember to do your part as a member of Christ's church.**

Bread of Life

Form groups of three. Give each group several slices of bread and instruct trios to create bread sculptures that represent "abundant life." For example, teenagers might shape their bread into a flower, a sun, or a cross.

When groups finish, place their sculptures on a baking sheet and toast them in an oven until they're golden brown. (If you don't have access to an oven in your church, borrow a toaster oven and bring it to your meeting.)

When the sculptures are toasted, have each group explain its creation. Then have volunteers read aloud *John 6:1-15, 22-35*. Have groups break apart their sculptures and eat them together as a symbol of their desire to let Christ's abundant life live within them.

Note: It's also enjoyable to sprinkle cinnamon and sugar on the sculptures before toasting them.

Burst My Balloon

Give kids identical balloons and ask them each to blow up their balloon to make it as large as possible. Tell kids that the person with the largest balloon will win $1.00. As kids blow up their balloons, walk around the room and encourage group members to keep blowing until a few balloons finally burst. When kids have stopped blowing up the balloons, measure them with a cloth measuring tape and award $1.00 to the winner. Then have kids form pairs to discuss these questions:

● **What were you thinking as you blew up your**

balloon?

- How did you decide when to stop blowing?
- How did you feel when some of the balloons burst?
- How is that like seeing people fail when they take risks?
- Which do you think is better—the fear of failure or the fear of being average? Explain.
- What do you think about when asked to take a risk in life?
- Is all risk-taking good? Why or why not?

Read aloud *Matthew 10:39* and *Philippians 3:7-9*. Ask:

- According to these verses, what risk does God ask Christians to take?
- Why do you think so few people actually take this risk?
- How can we encourage each other to risk for God?

Blow up one more balloon. With a marker, write on the balloon "I can risk for God because. . . " Form a circle and complete the sentence by saying something like "I can risk for God because God will be faithful to help me."

Then toss the balloon to someone else in the circle and have that person complete the sentence on the balloon. Repeat the process until everyone has had an opportunity to complete the sentence.

 # Chair Wars

Have kids pull their chairs into a tight circle, facing inward. Choose a volunteer to stand in the center of the circle. On "go," have the volunteer race to return to his or her seat. Instruct everyone else to prevent the volunteer from sitting by sliding into the empty chair before he or she can sit down. By sliding over, the group members will expose a different chair for the volunteer to try for. But have group members continue to slide into new seats to keep the volunteer from sitting for as long as they can.

Eventually the volunteer should manage to get a seat. When this happens, have the person on his or her right become the new volunteer. Continue for several rounds.

After the game, have volunteers read aloud *James 4:1-8*. Ask:

● **How did it feel to fight for a chair?**

● **How did it feel to fight to keep someone from getting a chair?**

● **How is this experience like or unlike what happens when we fight over getting the things we want?**

Read aloud *James 4:2-3* again. Ask:

● **Why do people sometimes neglect to ask God for the things they want or need?**

● **What are wrong motives for asking God for something? Explain.**

● **Based on** *James 4:1-8* **and your experience during our game, what advice would you give others about getting the things they want?**

Read aloud *James 4:7*. Say: **This week, instead of fighting each other to** *get* **things, let's focus on** *giving* **ourselves to God.**

Disabled Hands

Use this Bible study for a meeting about reaching out to disabled people.

Wrap a rubber band around the first three fingers of each person's writing hand. Have kids keep the rubber bands in place as they work together to create a mural about how Christians can show love to disabled people. Afterward have teenagers remove the rubber bands and discuss how it felt to be disabled while they created the mural. Ask:

● **What was your reaction to making a mural without the full use of your writing hand?**

● **How is the way you felt similar to the way a disabled person might feel?**

Form groups of no more than four and have them read *Acts 3:1-10*. Then have groups discuss these questions. Have the oldest person in each group report answers to the first question, the second oldest report answers to the second question, and so on. Ask:

● **How would you react to having a disability like the man in this story?**

● **What, besides physical ailments, disables a person?**

● **What might you have done differently if you'd been Peter or John in this story?**

● **How can Jesus use you to encourage a friend with a disability?**

Say: **You don't have to work a miracle to reach out to someone hampered by a disability—you just have to care. Let's practice caring this week.**

In His Steps

Bring an assortment of old shoes to a group meeting (you can borrow these from friends or simply dig deep into your own closets at home). Choose shoes that reflect a wide variety of activities; for example, hiking boots, work boots, cowboy boots, jogging shoes, high tops, leather shoes, loafers, dress shoes, or pumps. Make sure you also include one pair of men's sandals.

Tell kids they're going to play Shoe Detective. Form groups of three or four and give each group one or two pairs of shoes. Don't give out the sandals yet. Distribute paper and pencils. Say: **Based on the type of shoe and who it probably belonged to, write on your paper where that shoe might go during a typical day. For example, a hiking shoe might climb a mountain, wade through a stream, and get stuck in mud.**

When groups finish, have them explain their answers. Then set out the sandals. Say: **Sandals belonged to Jesus. Based on what you know of him, write on your paper where Jesus' sandals might go during a typical day.**

When groups are ready, have them tell what they wrote. Read aloud *John 12:26*. Ask:

● **What do you think it meant to follow Jesus in New Testament times?**

● **If Jesus came to earth today, where do you think he'd go? What do you think he'd do?**

● **How can you follow in Jesus' footsteps today?**

Then say: **This week, let's make our primary goal to go where Jesus would go and do what Jesus would do.**

Ladder of Success

Set out Popsicle sticks, glue, colored markers, and pens. Have each group member use the supplies to create and decorate a Popsicle-stick ladder to serve as a model for his or her own "ladder of success."

Encourage kids to make their ladders different from everyone else's and remind them that these ladders don't have to be straight. (See diagram for sample ideas.) Kids might create ladders with diagonal slats, ladders using only Popsicle-stick halves, or ladders with no middle slats. Kids might decorate their ladders with symbols of success or with a variety of colors to symbolize a variety of success. Tell everyone to leave the top rung on his or her ladder blank.

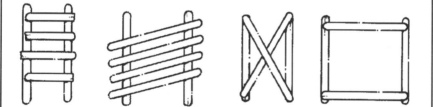

When kids finish, have them explain their creations to the group. Ask:

● **How did you feel about making your ladder different from everyone else's?**

● **How is building your own personal ladder of success like setting your own course for your life?**

● **Where do you want your ladder to end? What's one important success you'd like to achieve?**

Read aloud *Proverbs 4:25-27*. Ask:

● **How might the advice of** *Proverbs 4:25-27* **be compared to a ladder of success?**

● **With** *Proverbs 4:25-27* **in mind, what can you do this week that will help you move toward the goal you've chosen?**

Have kids write the Scripture reference "*Proverbs 4:25-27*" on the top rungs of their ladders. Encourage kids to hang their ladders on their bedroom walls as a constant reminder to keep their lives on the right course.

Lemon Identification

Before the meeting, use a marker to number enough lemons for each person in your group to have one. Place the numbered lemons in a sack.

At the meeting, form a circle and have teenagers put on blindfolds. Pass around the sack of lemons and have each person take one. With their blindfolds on, tell kids to carefully examine their lemons so they'll be able to recognize them again later in the meeting.

While kids are feeling their lemons, make a secret list noting which numbered lemon each person is holding. When kids feel like they're sufficiently intimate with their fruit, collect the lemons and set them all in a pile on a table.

Have kids remove their blindfolds, and have them take turns picking out their lemons. If kids were careful, they should each be able to pick out their original fruit. After everyone has chosen, check kids' picks against your secret list. Then ask:

● **What went through your mind when you found out that you'd have to identify your lemon without seeing it?**

● **What unique characteristics did you look for to help you identify your lemon?**

Form pairs. Have one partner read aloud *Psalm*

139:1-16, and the other summarize it in one sentence. Then have pairs discuss these questions:

- **How does your knowledge of your lemon compare to the way God knows you?**
- **Why do you think God is so interested in you?**
- **What's one unique and positive thing that God has created in you?**

Say: **From a distance it may seem that we're all the same—like a bag full of lemons. But just as each lemon is unique, God created us with special gifts and personalities. Because of that we can learn to see ourselves as special, unique members of God's family.**

 **Making Faces**

Form pairs. Give each pair a fistfull of rubber bands and a roll of cellophane tape. Have kids take turns using the rubber bands and tape to gently shape each other's face to reflect a specific emotion or attitude (see the illustration). Emotions and attitudes kids might use could be anger, fear, sadness, excitement, happiness, grief, arrogance, hatred, loneliness, and bitterness.

Note: The smaller the rubber bands, the better.

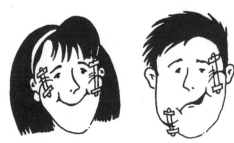

When pairs are finished, have them leave the rubber bands and tape in place as you call everyone together. Ask:

● **How does it feel to have the rubber bands and tape on your face right now?**

● **How is the irritation of the tape and rubber bands like the irritation of circumstances that try to affect our feelings and attitudes in life?**

● **Do you think it's possible to live above your circumstances so that your emotions remain more steady? Why or why not?**

Read aloud *1 Peter 1:3-9*, then ask:

● **What does this passage have to say about living under the weight of our circumstances?**

● **When have you experienced joy in tough circumstances?**

● **What do you think is the key to living joyfully in any circumstance?**

Have kids gently remove their tape and rubber bands. Say: **At times, it seems like life's circumstances try to shape our emotions and attitudes like the rubber bands and tape shaped our faces. But, as God's children, we can rely on God to help us live joyfully in any circumstance.**

 # Missing the Mark

Give kids each three sheets of scrap paper. Place a trash can in the middle of the room. Ask teenagers to wad the papers up and throw them into the trash can. Tell kids they only get one toss for each paper wad and that they must stand at least 15 feet away from the can.

After all the papers are tossed, gather everyone together and congratulate any who made all three shots.

Have kids stand as you ask the following questions. Give kids a few seconds to think after each question and tell them you'd like to hear lots of interesting responses. When one person shares an answer, kids who thought of the same answer and have nothing more to add can sit down. When everyone is seated, ask the next question and repeat the process. Ask:

● **How did it feel when you missed a shot?**

● **How is that like the way people feel when they fail in life?**

Say: **When we fail or mess up in our lives, we may feel angry or frustrated with ourselves. And we may feel like there's no second chance to try again. But we do have a second chance—through God's forgiveness.**

Have kids pick up the paper wads and put them into the trash can. Have volunteers read aloud *Romans 3:21-24* and *1 John 1:8-9*. Ask:

● **What thoughts about failure do you have after hearing this passage?**

● **Why do you think God is willing to give us second chances in life?**

● **What can you do this week to follow up on God's promise to give you a second chance?**

Lead the group in a prayer similar to this: **Lord, at times it's hard for us to "hit the targets" we have in our spiritual lives. Please let us all experience the power of your forgiveness as you help us live each new day for you. In Jesus' name, amen.**

My Mask, My Self

Give two paper plates to each person (the flimsy, inexpensive brands work best). Set out a supply of colored markers and colored pencils at each table.

On the first plate, have kids draw a picture of themselves as they think other people see them. Tell kids to include key words that add to the description. For example, someone who thinks everyone sees him or her as a funny person might draw a happy face and write "comedian" or "laughter" on the first plate. When kids finish, have them share their plates with everyone.

On the second plate, have kids draw a picture of how they see themselves. Once again, have them include key words to add to the description. When kids finish, have them share these pictures with everyone also. Then ask:

● **Which is the real you? Explain.**

Form discussion groups of no more than three. Have one or two people from each trio read aloud *1 Samuel 16:7* and *Psalm 139:1-6*. Have group members listen for what these verses say about wearing masks and hiding from God. After the readings, have groups each discuss what they heard and list their responses on a blank plate.

Have the person wearing the most blue in each group report their findings to the other trios. Then ask:

● **Of the two faces you drew, which one better reflects what God sees when he looks at you? Explain.**

● **What kinds of masks do we hide behind in our relationship with God?**

● **If God were to draw a paper-plate picture of you, how would it differ from the ones you drew? How would it be the same?**

● **What can we do this week to encourage open,**

honest communication with God and others?

Have kids complete this sentence prayer to close: "God, one thing I honestly want you to know is. . . " Kids might complete the sentence by saying things like "that I love you" or "that I need your forgiveness."

Rat Race

Mark a starting line with masking tape about three feet from one end of the room. Form teams of no more than four and have each team designate one person to be a "parent." Give each team a hymnal and three chocolate kisses. Line up the teams behind the starting line. Place a chair at the other end of the room opposite each team.

Say: **This is a rat race, and here's how it goes. Each team will balance a hymnal on the head of its parent. The parent will hold the chocolate kisses and walk to the other end of the room, circle the chair, and come back to the team. Still balancing the book, the parent will unwrap the chocolate kisses, place one kiss in the mouth of each team member, circle the chair again, and return to the team. OK, parents, heads up! Teams, balance your books.**

When a book is balanced on each parent's head, say "go." Encourage the teams to cheer their parents on. Each time a parent drops a book, have him or her stop and replace the book before starting again.

At the end of the race, give all the parents a round of applause. Ask the kids who sat on the sidelines:

● **How did it feel watching your parent struggle to finish the race?**

Ask the parents:

● **How did it feel balancing the book, running the**

race, and feeding your children?

Then ask the whole group:

● **How is this like what happens in your families in real life?**

Have the person born closest to Valentine's Day read *Colossians 3:12-15* for his or her team. Then have teams discuss these questions:

● **In what ways have you seen members of your family live out these verses?**

● **How do your everyday actions toward your family fulfill or not fulfill these verses?**

Say: **Oh—I almost forgot. I have rewards for all the parents.** Pass out 3×5 cards with stress-related illnesses written on them, such as "gastric ulcers," "migraine headaches," "nervous breakdowns," and "heart disease." Ask:

● **Are these the kinds of rewards real parents earn? Explain.**

● **How could following the instructions of** *Colossians 3:12-14* **help everyone in your family receive good rewards?**

Say: **Let's name practical ways you can support your parents to keep them from earning the kinds of rewards I just passed out. Each suggestion you give earns you a chocolate kiss.** Record kids' responses on a sheet of newsprint.

Say: **Giving and receiving support needs to be a two-way street. That's what keeps families working together. Tell other members of your team one thing you'll do this week to show consideration and understanding to someone in your family.**

 # Risky Business

Use masking tape to make a long, straight line on the floor. Have kids line up at one end of the masking tape line. Give everyone a paper plate.

Have each person balance his or her plate upside down on the palm of a hand. Pour several dried beans onto each person's plate. Then have kids each walk the straight line without spilling the beans. Afterward, ask:

● **How easy or difficult was it for you to walk the line without spilling the beans? Explain.**

Next, have kids line up again behind one end of the masking tape line. Beginning with the first person in the line, spin each teenager in place seven times. Then have them each immediately attempt to walk the line again without spilling the beans. Ask:

● **How easy or difficult was it for you to walk the line without spilling the beans? Explain.**

● **How was trying to keep from spilling the beans the second time like trying to live a healthy, productive life under the influence of alcohol or drugs?**

● **Why are people tempted to experiment with alcohol and drugs?**

Say: **Using drugs and alcohol is risky. The thrill of taking a risk is enough temptation for some people to try something. But just as being spun around took away your ability to walk straight, drugs and alcohol can take away your control and put you at great risk.**

Jesus may not have been tempted by drugs or alcohol, but he did face temptation. Let's see what we can learn from his temptation that can help us face the temptation to experiment with drugs or alcohol.

Make sure each person has a Bible, then form two groups. Have one group read Satan's lines and the other group read Jesus' lines in *Matthew 4:1-10*. Have a volunteer read the narration. Afterward, ask:

- **What were Jesus' temptations?**
- **How did Jesus respond?**
- **What does Jesus' response to temptation teach us about dealing with the temptations of drugs and alcohol?**
- **How important is it to seek God's help when you're tempted by the lure of drugs and alcohol? Explain.**

Say: **It takes a strong person to stand against the temptations of drugs and alcohol. Let's pray for each other to be strong people this week, month, year, and for the rest of our lives.**

Have kids spend a moment silently praying for a friend in the youth group to stand strong when facing the temptation to use drugs or alcohol.

 # Tool Time

Form groups of four or five. Give each group member a different hand tool, such as a hammer, screwdriver, pliers, tape measure, or wrench. Instruct kids to come up with a list of new and unusual ways to use their group's tool. For example, a hammer could be used as a paperweight, a screwdriver could be used as a drumstick, and a pair of pliers could be dressed up with cotton to become a little doll.

When kids are ready, have them present their new and unusual ideas to the other groups. When everyone is finished, ask:

- **How are these tools like people?**
- **How are they different?**
- **If we found so many different ways to use a simple tool, what does that say about how God can use us?**

Read aloud *Ephesians 2:10*. Say: **Each of us is**

made like a tool in that we each have a special purpose to fulfill in our lives. But we are much more than tools whether we have many talents or only a few, God can use us in an infinite variety of ways.

Water Into Wine?

Before the meeting, place one-half teaspoon of powdered grape-drink mix in a paper cup. Then place that cup somewhere in a stack of identical cups.

At the meeting, have volunteers read the story of Jesus at the wedding in Cana found in *John 2:1-11*.

Then take out the cups and a pitcher of water. Say: **Let's see if we can duplicate what Jesus did.**

Put the cups on a table in a row, not allowing kids to see the grape-drink mix in the bottom of one. Have volunteers take turns pouring water into the cups. When someone pours water into the cup with the drink mix, declare success.

Have kids finish pouring water into the other cups. Have kids gather around to see the filled cups. Ask:

● **What did you think when one of the cups filled up with grape drink?**

● **How is that like what the wedding guests might've thought when Jesus turned the water into wine?**

If kids haven't yet figured it out, tell them how you worked your miracle of turning the water into grape drink. Then ask:

● **What really makes something a miracle?**

● **What was the purpose of the miracles Jesus performed?**

● **What are some "everyday miracles," like flowers growing, that Jesus still works today? Why do** you think he does them?

Say: **In the Bible, Jesus performed miracles to bring glory to himself and to help others believe in him.**

But Jesus' greatest miracle still happens today. Through the power of his death and resurrection, Jesus gives new life to those who ask.

Have kids add grape-drink mix to the other cups. Then read *John 3:16* as a toast to Jesus and his miracle-working power.

LOW COST, NO COST
Parties and Projects

Inexpensive celebration and service ideas.

Another Friday night yawns by in your youth ministry. You'd like to have a great party for your kids, but you just can't think of an inexpensive way to pull one off. Saturday comes and goes. You know your kids would benefit from a time of serving others, but your kids are tired of old standards like free car washes and clean-up-the-church days.

So what do you do?

Simple. Pick out one of the fun, inexpensive parties or projects in this chapter and create a weekend your kids will remember for a lifetime!

Aid the Elderly (Project)

Plan a Saturday when your youth group will serve the elderly in your congregation. Obtain a list of people in need and call them to ask if they have any tasks your group can do around their houses; for example, housecleaning, weeding, or grocery shopping. Call only the number of people you think your group can accommodate that day.

Make a list of all the people you'll serve including their addresses and phone numbers, the jobs requested, an estimate of the time needed to finish the tasks, and the number of people needed to complete each job.

Have the kids meet at the church with sack

lunches. Give kids their assignments, then transport them to their assigned houses. When the kids are done, have them call you for transportation back to the church. When everyone returns, debrief group members on their projects with these questions:

● **What was it like to serve older people who can't do everything you can?**

● **What fun or funny things happened during your work?**

● **What stories did you hear from the people you served?**

● **What did you learn about growing old or being ill?**

● **What did you learn about serving others?**

Board Game Tournament (Party)

Use this party idea for an evening at winter retreats or camps when the weather won't allow outdoor events.

Gather popular games such as Monopoly, Trivial Pursuit, Pictionary, Scattergories, and Taboo. Set up game stations around the room with a game and necessary items (such as paper and pencils) at each station.

Have kids form pairs and join with other pairs at the game stations. Allow five minutes for setting up and going over rules. All games should be played by normal rules. For team games, such as Pictionary, have the two-person team play together. If it's an individual game, such as Monopoly, have kids play for themselves—but keep in mind that they'll be adding their scores to their partners' at the end of the game to determine the winning pair.

When teams are ready, allow them to play the

game for 15 to 30 minutes. Kids should complete as much of the game as possible in this time. When time is up, have everyone stop. Allow five minutes for the kids to add scores and determine which person or team has won. If no one has won yet, the person or team closest to winning is declared the winner.

Record each pair's performance, then have each pair find new pairs and a new game to play. Continue until kids have played each game. The pair winning the most games is the tournament champion.

Community Cleanup (Project)

Choose an area of town you'd like to adopt to keep clean for six months. Contact city officials to tell them of your idea. Let the city know you'd like to keep the chosen area clean of litter and graffiti. Ask if they'll provide paint to cover graffiti-filled walls or trash bags to fill with trash.

One Saturday each month, take a team of teenagers to the area to clean up for a couple of hours. When kids finish, take them back to the church for refreshments and a time of relaxation.

COST-CUTTING TIP

Cheap Entertainment—Instead of taking kids to expensive sporting events, introduce them to local college sports. Have kids choose a local team to support and enjoy the (usually) inexpensive entertainment of college sports.

Creation Celebration (Party)

Have teenagers plan a party for the younger children of the church emphasizing the wonderful variety and beauty of God's creation. Also, ask several parents to donate treats such as cookies and punch for the celebration.

Use tables to create a number of booths where group members present inexpensive, creation-related entertainment for the children to enjoy.

For example, booth entertainment might include examining an ant farm, petting a snake, or looking at empty birds' nests. You might also borrow some makeup and have a face-painting booth where teenagers paint animals on children's faces. Have animal-imitation contests to see who can do the best imitation of a mooing cow or a strutting rooster. Send children on a "stick hunt" to see who can find the most unusual twigs. End the party with a time of singing. Be sure to include fun songs about God's creative work such as "If I Were a Butterfly" and "Rise and Shine."

This party is especially fun during springtime.

Creative Dating (Party)

Tell teenagers to bring a date to this "creative dating party." Before the party, brainstorm ideas for safe, creative, and inexpensive dates; for example, wash a friend's car together, walk through a mall and window-shop a $1,000 shopping spree, or go to a playground and swing on the swings.

Print your ideas neatly on cards and place them in unmarked envelopes. As couples arrive, have them blindly choose a "creative date" envelope. Have couples follow the instructions on the cards they draw and go on their creative dates. Time the dates so kids can return to the church for a light snack and talk about what they did on their dates.

If you want to encourage group dating, write the same creative date idea on more than one card. Then, when couples choose the same creative date, have them go together.

In Search of a Square Meal (Project)

Prepare a list of grocery items needed to prepare a complete meal, including dessert. Make sure the meal is nutritious. Also, select a local agency that specializes in providing food for needy families to determine who the recipients of this project's work will be.

Form groups of four or five (include at least one adult in each group). Give each group a grocery sack, a copy of your grocery list, and a supply of your church's business cards. Instruct kids to go door to door, asking people to donate one or more items from the list. Tell kids to supply residents with a church business card so they'll know the project is legitimate. Have groups explain that the food is being collected to give to your chosen local agency.

Tell kids that they have two hours to collect the grocery items and that they may not purchase any items from the list themselves. Once groups are finished, or when the two hours are up, have kids return to the church to talk about the experience.

Have kids explain how it felt to go door to door,

how it felt to be rejected, and how it felt to be unable to complete their list without help from others. Discuss how all these feelings relate to the feelings of low-income families. Finish off the event by driving kids to the chosen agency to deliver the food.

Laundry Day (Project)

Many clothing-distribution centers need donated items to be washed before giving them to those in need. Larger organizations often have regular help to do this, but smaller groups usually have volunteers handle this part of their work. Contact local assistance centers, homes for unwed mothers, and distribution centers to volunteer your youth group's "laundry" skills.

Set aside one morning each month or quarter as "laundry day." Ask church members to volunteer their washers and dryers or ask them to provide small donations so kids can use a local laundromat.

Form work teams of two to four. Collect the unwashed clothes from the center, then have team members work together to sort the clothes, operate the machines, then fold and pack the clothes according to the clothing agency's instructions.

Ministers Waiting to Happen (Project)

Form a special group within your youth group called "MWTH" (pronounced "mwuth"). The name stands for "Ministers Waiting to Happen." One Saturday each month, have members of the MWTH team bring flowers, funny buttons, and chilled soft drinks to the church. Then take the MWTH team out in a van (if you don't have a church van, borrow one from a church member), and drive around the busier parts of town.

As you drive around town, have kids work together to choose individuals they want to encourage. It can be anyone—children at play, adults out shopping, even a homeless person on the street. Once they've chosen someone, stop the van and have the kids pile out and encourage the person by giving him or her a flower, a button, a hug, a cold drink, or a wish for a good day. Tell kids they may even offer to pray for the person on the spot, if it seems appropriate. Allow the kids to decide what to give to each person.

Each month, rotate the members of the MWTH team so all group members have a chance to participate. During the month, you might also encourage church members to donate soft drinks, buttons, or money for flowers and small gifts.

 **Night Before Prom Un-Prom (Party)**

Break up the tension of the local high school prom by organizing an "un-prom" for kids to attend a night (or a week) before their real prom. Have the un-prom start promptly at 8 p.m. and send out invitations with these instructions:

● The un-prom requires no attendance ticket. Admission price is one bag of chips, one can of soda, and one pillow.

● No one wearing nice clothes will be allowed to attend. The un-prom dress code requires all attendees to wear old, mismatched clothes. All outfits must be oversized and extremely comfortable.

● No dates are allowed. Singles only.

Before the un-prom, decorate a large meeting room with cheap or used decorations. Dim the lights and set up a table for kids' snacks. Bring several board games and prepare a few group games to start off the evening (see section 1: "Low Cost, No Cost *Games*," beginning on page 7 of this book, for ideas).

If possible, set up several chairs in one corner of the room and provide an instant-print camera for groups of kids to use to take mock prom pictures of themselves. Then just allow kids to relax, play games, and enjoy their snacks. Wrap up the evening with a lighthearted pillow fight.

Oldies Lip-Sync Party

Have an "oldies lip-sync party" featuring songs by famous singers and groups from the '50s and '60s such as Elvis Presley, Diana Ross and the Supremes, and the Beatles. Each person or group can pick one song they'd like to lip-sync. Then encourage kids to choreograph their songs.

Prepare a stage with a borrowed stereo system or boombox and mock sound equipment such as microphones and stands. Set up the room to resemble a fake '50s diner with tables, chairs, and a stage in the middle.

On the big night, have each group perform its song. Ask each young person to bring a plate of refreshments to share and have the church provide the drinks.

Recycled Party

Now that everyone's aware of recycling, organize a party with a recycling theme. Publicize the event by writing details on torn paper bags or the blank insides of cereal boxes and hanging them all around the church building.

Admission for the event is two or more recyclable items such as aluminum cans, plastic milk jugs, food boxes, or glass jars.

Before the event, have kids form teams and use

the recyclable materials they'll bring to create new games; for example, Pin the Foil on the Cereal Carton, Aluminum Can Knock-down, or Toss the Cardboard Squares into a Glass Jar.

At the party, have kids explain their games and play them. Have teams award prizes such as packets of recycled paper, a previously worn sweater, or a six-pack of soft drinks (the cans and bottles can be recycled).

Something Wooded This Way Comes (Party)

Here's a great way to make a bonfire night really exciting. Make simple tickets for the bonfire (one ticket for every four people). Cut each ticket into five pieces. Make sure you cut up all the tickets in the same way.

Recruit several adult volunteers to act as "the missing pieces" for the event. Encourage these adults to disguise themselves in black costumes before the event.

Drive to a secluded, wooded area near a bonfire site. Form groups of four and give each group four pieces of a ticket. Distribute the "fifth pieces" equally among the adult volunteers.

Explain to kids that no group is allowed near the bonfire without a whole ticket, so each group will have to recover its missing piece from the appropriate adult. Tell kids that the adult volunteers will give up their missing pieces without a fight, but the catch is that kids must find the adults first.

Send the adult volunteers into the woods to hide (make sure they have flashlights). After about five minutes, release the groups to find the adults and retrieve the missing pieces of their tickets.

While the kids are searching for people in the woods, prepare the bonfire. Allow the first groups back to be the first to roast marshmallows and enjoy the fire. When everyone has returned, lead the group in a time of sharing and singing worship songs.

Storm Troopers (Project)

Have group members sign up to be "storm troopers." Storm troopers shovel walks and driveways for people in your church or neighborhood who need assistance. Announce this free service at the beginning of winter through church bulletins and local newspaper ads. Have those needing assistance call the church to be placed on a shoveling route. Make sure you sign up only as many people as your storm troopers can reasonably help. It's far better to say no to someone who wants the service than to say yes and fail to provide it.

Form teams of no more than four young people, assigning an adult sponsor to each team (it's OK if one adult sponsors more than one team). Have each team choose one member as its captain. This person will be responsible for calling all members during snow storms to let them know when they'll begin shoveling.

Give each team a route for the

COST-CUTTING TIP

Money Assumptions—Never assume kids can afford whatever your activities cost. If you do, you give the impression that all your kids have money readily available. Avoid making announcements such as "Bring $20 for admission to the concert." Instead, acknowledge when a trip or activity will be expensive. Try to offset at least some of the cost with fund-raisers.

snow season—not more than four homes per team. After a storm, teams can quickly clean the walks and drives of the homes on their routes. Ask the adult sponsors to regularly check on the kids' work and to help teams if they have trouble.

10-Year Reunion (Party)

Invite kids to a party during which they'll become the people they envision themselves being 10 years from now. After the kids gather, take them through a "time warp"—a dark hallway—where they proceed 10 years into the future. Decorate the party area with streamers and balloons.

Ask kids to bring their current high school yearbooks as nostalgia items. Have kids fill out "10-Year Reunion" handouts (p. 61) and use them as the basis of their conversations with their "former" classmates. Serve refreshments, then take kids back through the time warp to the present day.

10-Year Reunion

Welcome to your 10-year class reunion! It's nice to see you after all these years. It'll be great to catch up on all the news with your classmates. Take a few minutes to fill out this information sheet. After you've filled out the sheet, share all your news with your old classmates.

Name

My current job

Family status

The car I'm driving

Where I live

Post-high-school training

Places I've visited

My greatest accomplishment since high school

Favorite class memory

Goals for the next 10 years

LOW COST, NO COST
"Out of Bounds" Ideas

Ideas for youth groups away from church grounds.

Youth ministry doesn't end when your kids walk out of the church doors. You can use camps, retreats, resources in your community, and even time spent traveling to continue your ministry "out of bounds," or off church grounds. Use the fun ideas in this section to help you get started.

Afflicted Bowling Night

Check with local bowling alleys to discover the best rates for group bowling, then take your teenagers out for an "afflicted bowling night."

Before going to the bowling alley, designate fake afflictions for each of your kids such as being blind, having a broken leg, or having a broken arm. Depending on the affliction, bind or cover that part of each person's body so he or she will be unable to use it.

After each person has been given an affliction, go bowling together. Encourage kids to help each other as they play. Tell them ahead of time that the only way anyone can win is for everyone in the group to score 75 or more.

After the game, commend kids for their efforts. Then read aloud *Galatians 6:2*. Have kids discuss their experience and what they can learn from "afflicted bowling" and *Galatians 6:2* to help them in real life.

Exodus Week

Plan a weeklong summer camp focusing on the book of Exodus.

For fun, during the first meeting, have the group come up with 10 commandments everyone must follow during the retreat. They could be funny (thou shalt do a somersault before each meal) and/or serious (thou shalt not speak rudely to anyone here).

Allow the group to create penalties for lawbreakers; for example, a lawbreaker must go last in line for his or her next meal or must compliment everyone in the group.

During the week, try these activities:

● **Pharaoh's Plummeting Plunge**—If your camp location has a pool, have a diving contest. Award prizes for the dive most likely to part the waters (biggest splash) and the dive most likely to climb Mount Zion (highest bounce).

● **Amalekite Ambush**—Gather in an open field and form two teams, the Israelites and the Amalekites. When you (Moses) have your arms up, the Israelites chase the Amalekites. Those that are tagged must sit on the edge of the playing area. When your arms are down, the Amalekites try to tag the Israelites. Fold your arms when teams need a chance to regroup—or when you need a rest! The team with the last remaining person wins.

Note: This game can also be a lot of fun when played in a pool.

● Rent Cecil B. DeMille's movie *The Ten Commandments* and show it to your group. (Remember, you may need permission to

COST-CUTTING TIP

Movie Tickets—Contact your local movie theater and find out if they give volume discounts on the purchase of movie tickets. Many theaters are happy to sell a quantity of movie tickets at reduced prices. Plan ahead for your next movie event so you and your teenagers can each save a couple dollars.

show the movie to your group.) Serve "manna" (popcorn—it'll seem like manna when it's all over the floor after the movie!). Then discuss how the movie is different from the biblical account in Exodus.

● Hike to a secluded area for a picnic. Talk about how the Israelites must have felt hiking around in the wilderness, unsure of where they were really going and having to trust God for food, water, and protection.

 # Giveaway Day

Have kids spend a month gathering household items from friends, neighbors, and their own houses for a "giveaway day." Encourage kids to collect quality items, not junk. Kids might collect clothes, tools, children's toys, used books, electronic equipment, puppies, kittens, even a refrigerator (if one's available).

On the designated day, borrow a truck or two from congregation members and have kids load everything they've collected into the trucks. Then drive around town (kids can follow in cars), stopping at shopping centers, parks, or other church parking lots to set up roving "giveaway stations." Offer the items in your truck(s) free to anyone who wants them. Limit giveaways to one item per person.

Give away as many items as you can. Donate leftover items to your local Salvation Army or Goodwill store.

In Another Land Retreat

Plan an overnight retreat in which kids do every-thing according to what time it is in a different country. Set up a schedule that reflects the time of day in that country and plan activities around that country. For example, if you're on standard time and planning a retreat based on the United Kingdom, you might begin the retreat at 1:00 p.m. MST Satur-day (8:00 p.m. Saturday, UK time), have lights out at 5:00 p.m. MST (midnight, UK time), and have breakfast at Midnight (7:00 a.m. Sunday, UK time). Have kids adjust their watches to match UK time for the entire event.

Plan activities and meals that reflect the country you choose for this retreat. For example, if you choose China, have kids use chopsticks and eat Chinese food. If you choose Ireland, play Irish music during the retreat. If you choose Spain, have kids learn to play castanets.

After the retreat, plan on kids suffering from "jet lag." Discuss how experiencing another culture is like or unlike their retreat experience.

Make this an annual event so kids can look for-ward to visiting a new country each year.

Junkyard Sculptures

Take kids to a local junkyard. Equip kids with work gloves and arrange with the yard opera-tors to allow kids to search the junk heaps for inter-esting scraps to be used to create junk sculptures. (Most junkyards will let you take your pick of unus-able junk for a small fee—or even for free.) Caution kids against picking scrap that's too large to fit in a car. Once each person has collected several pieces of scrap, gather kids together and drive to a nearby park.

At the park provide wire, wire cutters, glue, and duct tape and instruct kids to use their junk to create several small sculptures. The sculptures can be anything, as long as they incorporate all or most of the scrap pieces. Encourage kids to be creative and to try to create sculptures that communicate positive messages.

When kids are finished, hold a private art show in the park. Have kids present and explain their sculptures. Have them include explanations of what they meant their sculptures to communicate. When kids are finished, discuss together how kids' work with the metal scraps could be compared to God's work in people's lives. Explain that although people aren't junk, they are often broken or rusted, and God makes beautiful works of art out of brokenness. Let kids take their sculptures home to remind kids that they're works of art in God's hands.

Love Tour

Give your teenagers a glimpse of another side of life by taking them on a love tour.

Visit an AIDS hospice or a hospital ward for the terminally ill. Notify the hospice or hospital in advance that you would like to visit. Arrange for a short question-and-answer session with someone who works there. Take along small gifts for the patients and prepare kids to be ready to pray for patients if it's appropriate.

Afterward, debrief the experience with your group back at the church. Discuss kids' feelings and impressions. End with prayer for those you have visited.

 # Mall Hunt

Use this fun idea the next time you take your group to the mall. Ask several of your adult volunteers to disguise themselves and meet with you before kids arrive. Give each disguised volunteer a sheet of self-adhesive stickers to give to kids who see through the disguise. (Make sure each person has a different sticker design.) Tell volunteers all they have to do is roam from store to store in the mall while the kids seek them out. Specify a location in the mall for the adult volunteers to meet when the game is over.

Send your volunteers to the mall and wait for kids to arrive at your regular meeting place. When everyone has arrived, form teams of three and give each team a sheet of paper. Say: **We're going to the mall for a sticky kind of treasure hunt. All the adult volunteers have disguised themselves and are at the mall. Each of them has a secret sticker that you must get to win the treasure. Your team's job is to locate each of the disguised sponsors and collect all the secret stickers on your sheet. The first team to accomplish this task wins.**

Take kids to the mall. Designate a location for kids to meet when they're finished. Tell kids to return within one and a half hours whether they're finished or not. Then start the treasure hunt.

When the hunt is over and a winner is declared, have everyone (including sponsors) enjoy an ice-cream treat together.

Mall Trivia

To prepare for this event, spend an afternoon at your local mall making a list of unique characteristics in store window displays; for example, the number of mannequins in a popular clothing store, the number of stuffed bears in a toy-store window, and the number of professional sports teams represented in an athletic-store display. Then make a list of questions based on the information you collected; for example, "Which store has four mannequins wearing red and white polka dots?"; "How many stuffed bears are in the window of the toy store?"; "What sports teams are represented in the window display of the sports store?"; and "In which store is there a salesperson named Mindy? (10 bonus points if you can get her signature)."

Assign point values to the questions according to their difficulty and photocopy your list of questions. The day of the event, take your kids to the mall. Form teams of three and give each team a list of questions. Give them one hour to find the answers to as many questions as possible (late teams lose 1 point for every minute they're late). The team with the most points wins.

COST-CUTTING TIP

Gas Savings—When planning events for your group, consider locations that can easily be reached by biking, walking, or riding public transportation. This saves money (and helps keep the environment clean, too).

Mystery Leadership Retreat

Use this overnight retreat idea to draw your youth leadership team together and get their input for your activities.

Make all the arrangements without letting the kids know what you'll be doing. Arrange with a member of your church to borrow his or her house overnight. When kids arrive at the church, blindfold them and take a long route to the house. Don't remove the blindfolds until kids are inside the home.

Once the blindfolds are off, set up "camp"—create tents using blankets and chairs. After having kids prepare and eat a meal together, start your program.

Here's an overview of how the retreat might go:

1. Have kids each find an object in the house that's most like them and have them explain why they chose the object they did.

2. Ask kids to share their expectations of being a leader.

3. Pray together, asking God to help each person be the best leader possible.

4. Spend the rest of the evening playing small group games your teenagers will enjoy. (See section 1: "Low Cost, No Cost *Games*," beginning on page 7.)

5. The next morning have a breakfast of cereal, milk, and fruit. Lead kids in a devotion on following Jesus as leader. (See the devotion on page 34 in section 2, "In His Steps.")

6. Hold a foot-washing time in which either you wash kids' feet and affirm each person as you do, or kids affirm partners as they wash each other's feet.

7. Take a break—plant flowers for your hosts as a way to thank them for allowing your group to use the house (get permission from the hosts before the retreat).

8. After a simple lunch, spend the afternoon planning your events for the year. Then clean up the home and drive back to the church.

On the Road With Paul

Plan a retreat based on Paul's travels in the book of Acts. Bring along inexpensive props and costumes and, at various times during the retreat, re-enact some of the exciting events listed here:

- The Stoning of Stephen—*Acts 7:54–8:1*
- Paul's Conversion—*Acts 9:1-19*
- Stoned!—*Acts 14:8-20*
- In Prison—*Acts 16:16-34*
- Raising the Dead—*Acts 20:7-12*
- Shipwrecked!—*Acts 27:13-44*
- Preaching Jesus Christ—*Acts 28:23-30*

After each re-enactment, discuss the effect the event had on Paul's life and his faith in God. Examine how we can learn from Paul's example and his experience.

Have kids sleep in tents (Paul was a tent maker) and take long hikes (Paul likely walked hundreds of miles on his missionary journeys). For fun, give everyone a special "Paul's friend" name for the retreat, such as Barnabus, Timothy, Priscilla, and Aquila. Many of Paul's friends are listed in the farewell sections of his letters.

COST-CUTTING TIP

Freebies—Plan your outings so the majority are free. Cut down on the usual trips to zoos, museums, bowling alleys, and other places that charge fees to use their facilities. Kids can have fun together in lots of places that don't charge anything. Try relay races and water games in a park. Tour TV stations, police headquarters, and factories as well.

Prayer Field Trip

Take your group on a prayer field trip away from where you live. Go to a nearby city, to a neighborhood across town, or into the country. As you go, have kids develop lists of things to pray about.

For example:

● Kids might look for things that inspire them to worship God, such as majestic mountains, church buildings, or flowers growing in a garden.

● Kids might look for things that remind them that we need to confess our sins to God. X-rated theaters, litter by the freeway, or crude bumper stickers on other cars could all be reminders.

● Kids might look for things to thank God for, such as friends' homes, food that's available in grocery stores, or beautiful scenery.

● Kids might look for needs to ask God's help in filling, such as people living in poverty, victims of crime, people in hospitals, and farmers.

When kids are ready, stop and have group members take turns praying for the people and things they wrote on their lists.

Pseudo White-Water Rafting

Here's a fun way to help your kids cool off in the summer—pseudo white-water rafting!

To prepare for this activity, you'll need heavy rope, yarn, eight to 10 speed cones or chairs, several large buckets or small trash cans, and a water source.

Tell kids to dress to get wet, then take them to a

large grassy field, park, or back yard. If possible, use a location on a sloping hill. Mark off a winding "river" course through the field with yarn and place your "rocks" (the speed cones or chairs) at random throughout the course (see diagram). Explain that kids are going to have the chance to "raft" down the river in teams.

Form teams of no more than six. Use rope to tie a snug but comfortable loop around the team members. Tell team members that they may not let go of the rope at any time during the race. Station other group members with buckets of water at each cone or chair. Their job is to douse the rafters as they go by.

When the first team is ready, place team members at the starting line and explain the route they must take to reach the finish. Time their race. When the team reaches the finish line, provide towels and let another team try to beat the first team's time.

Once all the teams have run the course, allow teams to go again.

But this time blindfold everyone except one team leader in each racing team. The team leader must direct his or her team along the route and warn them of rocks (and buckets of water).

The team with the best combined time wins.

Ties That Bind

This quick game can be used any time your group travels or gets stuck waiting for a bus or plane.

Explain that you'll call out a category. When you do, kids must find others who meet the criteria of the category and sit together on the floor. Tell everyone to add the number of people sitting in that group to their individual scores. Have kids keep track of their own scores. The person with the highest individual score wins.

Here are categories you could call out:
- find everyone whose favorite brand of soft drink is the same as your own,
- find everyone who is wearing the same color as you are,
- find everyone who has the same number of brothers and sisters as you,
- find everyone whose favorite band (or performer) is the same as yours,
- find everyone who was born in the same month you were, and
- find everyone whose favorite Disney movie is the same as yours.

After going through several categories, congratulate the winner with a free soft drink (make sure it's the right brand!).

Wacky-Tongue Scavenger Hunt

Prior to this activity, ask church members to loan instant-print cameras and donate film to your group. Then create a list of people from your church, neighborhood, or community who wouldn't mind having fun participating in a silly activity. Write down each person's name and occupation. Assign each listed person a point rating according to difficulty of access. For example, your senior minister may be fairly easy to approach, so assign him or her 10 points, but a mayor may be worth 100 points.

Form as many teams as you have cameras. Tell kids that the object is to get the people on your list to stick out their tongues while kids take their pictures with the instant-print cameras. Encourage creativity by awarding 100 bonus points to the team with the picture of the strangest tongue. Pictures should be head shots only.

Allow teams a few minutes to plan their strategies, then send kids out to get their wacky-tongue pictures. Have everyone meet back at the church in an hour, then total the teams' points. For added fun, play tongue-twister games and eat colorful foods (like red Popsicles!).

Close by using *James 3:1-12* as the basis for a brief devotion.

Walk Rally

Create a walk rally—a no-car version of a car rally. Pick a place where you want to begin your rally, such as the church. Also choose a place where kids will end up, such as a local ice-cream shop, pizza place, or park. Be sure only the committee planning the rally knows the final destination.

Plan a route from your starting location to your final meeting place. Make up clues that provide directions for kids. For example, let's say you want the students to go west on "Harbor Street." A clue could be "face the setting sun on the street where the boats come to rest." Make the clues challenging but not so difficult that the game isn't fun.

On the day of the rally, have kids form groups of five. Give each group a clue sheet and a sealed envelope containing the actual directions to the final destination just in case anyone gets lost. Send the first group on its way. Let the remaining groups go five to 10 minutes apart after that (this way the groups can't follow one another). Track the beginning and ending times of each group to see who finishes the rally the fastest.

Water Gun Putt-Putt

The next time you want to take your group out for a round of miniature golf, try this fun alternative. Before the event, ask kids to each bring a water gun (they can bring any type of water gun they want—just don't tell them what it's for) and a pingpong ball with their name on it.

After everyone arrives, car pool to a nearby park or grassy field. Lay several glass tumblers on their sides all around the park (or field) to create a mock miniature golf course.

Explain to group members that they're going to play regular miniature golf, except they'll use their water guns instead of clubs, their pingpong balls as golf balls, and the glass tumblers as the holes. Kids will only be able to move the balls by squirting them, and each squirt counts as one stroke. All the other rules are the same.

Once everyone understands the rules, form groups of no more than four and have kids begin.

If you don't have a handy water source nearby, bring a couple of buckets with you and periodically fill them with water from a restroom.

When the game is over, award the winner(s) a miniature water gun or a plastic golf club (these are available at minimal cost from most toy stores).

COST-CUTTING TIP

Travel Tip—Traveling with teenagers can be expensive. Consider camping along the way (if the weather allows) or staying in churches (contact your denominational headquarters for a list of churches in the towns you'll be visiting).

Note: You can also play this game at an actual miniature golf course. Before the event contact the manager of the course and tell him or her what you're planning. The manager may be willing to reserve time after hours at a discounted rate for your group.

LOW COST, NO COST
Holiday Ideas

Creative ways to observe special days
throughout the year.

At times it's easy to get caught unprepared for the various holiday seasons. This year use this section to help you get ready. It's filled with ideas to help your youth group observe special days throughout the year in new and exciting ways.

All-Holiday Party

When your teenagers are hungering for a holiday, but it seems the nearest one is months away, then it's time for an all-holiday party.

Tell group members to each come to this party dressed in a costume (or seasonally appropriate clothing) that represents their favorite holiday. For example, one person may come dressed as a wise man for Christmas, and another may come dressed in red and white hearts for Valentine's Day. Have each person bring a dessert that's traditional for his or her holiday, such as green clover-shaped cookies for Saint Patrick's Day or pumpkin pie for Thanksgiving. Dress up the room with decorations from past holiday parties.

Begin the event with a countdown to the new year. Then provide heart-shaped paper and have the kids each fill out an anonymous valentine by writing something about themselves that no one else would know. Shuffle the valentines, then redistribute them to the group. Have kids each find their "sweetheart" (the person who wrote the valentine) by asking each other yes or no questions about what the valentine says.

Next, play Saint Patrick's Day Tag—those wearing green are "It." Have the Its run around and try to pinch everyone who isn't wearing green. The last person to get pinched wins the game.

Move to the Easter portion of your evening by having partners read *1 Corinthians 15:12-23* and discuss how their lives would be different if Jesus had not been raised from the dead. Allow time for pairs to report their thoughts to the group.

For Independence Day, play flag games such as flag football or capture the flag. Afterward, drink a lemonade toast to celebrate the freedom God's given to American society.

For Halloween, have kids play Trick or Treat! at the dessert table. Tell them that to get some dessert, each person has to say, "Trick or treat!" then do a trick for the servers. For example, kids might sing a song, wiggle their ears, or recite *Mary Had a Little Lamb* as they hop on one foot.

To celebrate Thanksgiving, have teenagers take turns telling three reasons they're thankful for the youth group and its members.

Close out the party by singing Christmas carols and reading the story of Jesus' birth in *Luke 2*.

New Year's Day People Parade

This activity is a takeoff on the parades held every New Year's Day. The difference is that instead of roses and cars being the main ingredients, it's the people that matter most.

Form "float" teams of five or fewer. Tell teams the goal is to transform one member of each team into a living, breathing float for a New Year's Day parade. Teams will do this by decorating that person in the most outlandish way possible.

Let kids know they'll have until New Year's Day to plan and prepare their floats. The only rule is that teams can't spend more than $5 for decorations. Encourage kids to rely on common items for their "raw materials." Here are common materials kids can use:

- magazine and newspaper pictures
- yarn or rope
- cardboard
- popcorn strung on thread
- old clothes and jewelry
- tissue or toilet paper
- paper towels or napkins
- light bulbs
- Halloween masks
- Christmas lights
- artificial plants
- confetti
- Christmas tree ornaments
- garland
- aluminum foil

On New Year's Day, have teams meet in the morning to finish their floats and get them in line for the people parade. Invite families from the church to join in the festivities.

When ready, play silly background music as each float passes in front of the rest of the group. Declare winners in the following categories: most creative, best use of materials, best highlighting of the nose, most unusual, most materials used, and most aesthetically pleasing.

Congratulate your winners, then serve refreshments and watch a football game to end your time together.

Valentine's Day "Humming" Beacon

Here's a great activity for a meeting around Valentine's Day.

Blindfold two people, a guy and a girl, and place them on opposite sides of the room. Spin them around to disorient them, then explain that they must find each other within 60 seconds or they'll be doomed to eternal peril. If they do find each other within one minute, they'll find eternal happiness. Tell them that although they may not say anything, the rest of the group will help them by humming louder when they get closer together and softer when they're far apart.

After the first pair has accomplished the task, congratulate their efforts, and repeat the game with two new volunteers. This time hold up a secret sign that reads "do the opposite" so that the group is humming louder when the volunteers are moving away from each other.

After a few minutes, have the second pair remove their blindfolds, then show them the secret sign. Play several rounds changing the rules at random. See how long it takes for pairs to figure out whether the group is bringing them together or pulling them apart.

Afterward, lead the group in a discussion exploring the influence others have on our choices in relationships. Use *Romans 12:1-2* as a basis for the discussion.

Tie the Knot on Valentine's Day

This Valentine's Day, try this new twist on a well-known game. Have kids form a circle and join hands. Then challenge kids to create a knot with their hands and bodies without letting go of each other's hands. Encourage kids to crawl over, under, or around each other at random—whatever it takes to become as tangled as possible.

Once everyone is super-tangled together, ask:

● **What was fun about getting all tangled like this? Explain.**

● **How is a dating relationship like this knot we've created?**

Have kids untangle themselves without releasing each other's hands. Ask:

● **Was it hard to untangle yourselves without letting go of each other? Why or why not?**

● **How is untangling our knot like breaking up with a boyfriend or girlfriend?**

Read aloud *Romans 13:8* and *Hebrews 13:1*. Ask:

● **What's the best way to handle a breakup? What's the worst way to handle it?**

● **What can we learn from these Scriptures and our knots to help us handle our dating relationships in a way that honors God?**

Carry a Cross for Easter

This Easter challenge your group with this life-changing idea. Find a wooden beam that's approximately 6 feet long, 6 inches wide, and 6 inches high (the beam should weigh between 30 and 40 pounds). Check with a local lumberyard for free wood scraps or ask the manager if he or she can donate the wooden beam to your group (make sure to explain why you need it). You'll also need rope.

One week before Easter, gather your group together and show them the beam. Explain that Jesus had to carry a beam like this as he walked the road to Calvary—the place he was crucified.

Read aloud *Mark 8:34-38*. Tell kids that this week they're going to have the opportunity to proclaim their choice to follow Jesus and raise their friends' awareness about the true meaning of Easter.

During the week, have kids gather on the edge of their school grounds during lunch break. (If your youth group members go to several schools, have kids gather at a different school at the end of each school day.) Each day have a different volunteer strap the beam across his or her shoulders then walk once around the perimeter of the school grounds. Have the rest of the group follow behind the person to offer encouragement and physical help, if needed.

By the third day, everyone in the school will be talking about what your group is doing. Tell kids not to explain what they're doing unless asked directly. If people do ask, have kids explain their actions and invite others to a celebration at your church on Easter night.

The day before Easter, cut the beam into pieces and place them on top of a pile of wood in an open area outside your church.

At the Easter celebration, display a banner that reads "He's alive!" or "He is risen!" Have group members act out or read the story of Christ's death and resurrection. Then burn the beam as a symbol of Christ's victory over death. Have kids pray together that everyone at their school can

learn the truth about Jesus. After the prayer, celebrate the Resurrection with music, singing, and a
marshmallow roast.

Easter Surprise

Here's an innovative way to bring home the message of Easter.

Before a youth group meeting, prepare the youth
room (or another available room) for a surprise
party. Make the room dark—so dark that kids won't
be able to see the party decorations. Use black plastic to cover the windows, seal cracks with black
tape, and cover any other openings that allow light
into the room.

Leave the front of the room empty and open—
you'll gather kids in the dark there later. Fill the
rest of the room with colorful balloons, streamers,
confetti, and a sign declaring that Jesus is alive. Set
up a table with snacks and get a cassette player
ready to play lively Easter music. Then turn out the
lights and leave the room.

When it's time to start, meet kids outside the door
to the youth room but don't let anyone enter. Gather
the group and say: **For this activity, we need to be
serious and meditative. We're going to visit Jesus'
tomb. Let's be quiet and reflect on the sacrifice Jesus
made on the cross.**

Lead kids silently into the front of the darkened
room and have them sit in a circle on the floor. Light
a candle—don't let kids turn on the lights. Have kids
take turns passing the candle around the circle as
they complete this sentence: "To me, Jesus' death
means. . . "

Afterward, say: **Let's take a moment to thank
Jesus for dying on the cross for us.**

Have kids close their eyes and pray silently for 30 seconds. When time is up, blow out the candle, turn on the lights, and yell: **Surprise! Jesus has risen from the dead! Let's celebrate!**

Turn on the music and have kids enjoy the snacks. Encourage kids to toss the balloons and streamers around the room in celebration. Then have kids form a circle and ask:

● **What were you thinking when I led you into this room?**

● **How was the surprise of this celebration like the surprise of Jesus' resurrection?**

● **What does Jesus' resurrection mean to you?**

After everyone has enjoyed their time of celebration, gather kids in a circle and read aloud *Matthew 28:1-7* to close.

Freedom to Choose on Independence Day

At one of your regular youth group meetings around Independence Day, set up four tables in the room with basic arts-and-crafts supplies, such as newsprint, paint, paintbrushes, markers, pipe cleaners, and paper cups.

Form four groups and have each group gather around a table. Let each group designate one person to be the artist and send that person into a separate room.

Tell kids that the artists will return and begin projects with the available supplies. Everyone else's job will be to convince his or her group's artist to stop or change the project.

While the artists are in the other room, have a

volunteer assign each artist an art project. Ideas for art projects might be to paint or draw a self-portrait, make a sculpture of a flag, or create a paper-cup castle.

At the appropriate time tell the artists to return to their tables and use the available supplies to complete their assigned projects. Tell them the project doesn't have to be pretty or meaningful—it just has to fulfill the assignment. Tell artists that other group members may not like what they're doing but to do it anyway.

Once the art projects are underway, go from table to table and secretly encourage group members to badger their artist to stop the project or to do some other project that the other group members suggest. However, make sure the group members don't touch the artist's work or begin building anything themselves.

When the artists are finished, or after several minutes, gather everyone together and ask:

● **How did it feel to try to finish the art project under such opposition? Explain.**

● **How did it feel to badger the artist like you did? Explain.**

Re-form the four groups. Have groups read *2 Timothy 3:10-14* and *Matthew 5:10-12*, then summarize the verses in one sentence. Next have groups discuss these questions:

● **How is being an artist in this experience like trying to live as a Christian in our world today? Explain.**

● **How do other people—friends included—try to take away or hinder your freedom to live as a Christian?**

● **Is freedom to live as a Christian worth fighting for? Why or why not?**

● **When have you had to fight for the freedom to live out your Christian faith?**

● **How did that affect your faith?**

● **What's one thing you can do this summer to**

freely express your Christian faith in your daily life?

Halloween-Mummy Game Night

During the Halloween season invite kids to come to a game night at your church. Tell kids their ticket into the event is a roll of toilet paper. Once kids have arrived, form groups of four or fewer, distribute tape, and have kids mummify each other by wrapping their partners in toilet paper from head to toe. Make sure kids wrap each other's arms and legs individually so kids can still walk and use their arms.

Once everyone is mummified, tell kids you're going to lead them in several games such as Hop-scotch, Volleyball, Tag, and Hide-and-Seek. Explain that the goal of the evening is not so much to win the games as it is for kids to keep themselves mummified. The teenagers with the most intact toilet paper on their bodies at the end of the evening win a Grand Mummy Award (a roll of toilet paper impaled on a gold stick).

Once the games begin, kids may not use any more tape to reinforce their mummy wrappings, although they can stuff the wrappings in their clothes to keep them attached.

End the evening with a short devotion that tells how people who are spiritually dead can find new life in Jesus Christ.

Thanksgiving Hike

Instead of the typical Thanksgiving meal, have kids prepare lunches and go on a hike in your neighborhood. As kids hike, have them point out things they're thankful for along the way.

Kids might identify specific items they see or items that represent something else. For example, someone might point out a gas station and say, "I'm thankful that the Holy Spirit fills us with fuel to keep going in tough times." Or someone might point to a nursing home and say, "I'm thankful for my grandparents."

During the lunch break, have kids say what makes them thankful for each other. Make the whole experience a time for reflection and appreciation for what God has done in their lives.

Christmas Caroling for Nonsingers

For those groups that don't like to sing Christmas carols, plan an evening of "reverse" carols. During this event kids visit choir members' homes and ask the choir members to sing a Christmas carol to your group. Choose only those choir members who wouldn't mind the strangeness of this activity and who would be bold enough to sing carols to a group of smiling kids.

Or have kids take along a portable cassette player and lip-sync the carols from home to home. Kids can have fun choosing the sound they want for their group (anything from the Mormon Tabernacle Choir to the Chipmunks).

Finally kids could just as easily read the Christmas carols in unison rather than sing them. While it may seem strange at first, people will enjoy hearing the words of the carols without the music getting in the way of the meaning.

Christmas Rush–Not!

Here's a fun and practical Christmas idea for your youth group. Early in December have your teenagers gather at the church for a day of shopping and play. Once everyone has arrived, car pool to a local mall or shopping center and set teenagers loose to do their Christmas shopping. Remind kids that they're not shopping for a gift exchange at the church, but for their own gift exchanges with family and friends on Christmas day.

While you're at the mall, have parents volunteer to decorate the youth group room at the church for a Christmas party. Encourage them to use inexpensive decorating supplies such as crepe paper, newsprint posters, and homemade confetti. Ask parents to donate snacks for the party as well.

In addition to treats and drinks, ask parents to set up a wrapping table with a collection of Sunday comics (to use as present-wrapping paper), tape, scissors, and inexpensive bows (department stores usually sell bags of these at minimal cost).

After a few hours at the mall, have kids check in at a prearranged spot for lunch. If necessary allow more time for kids to finish up their shopping. Then bring kids back to the church.

Back at the youth group room, play Christmas music and allow kids to enjoy the party your volunteers have set up. Let kids use the supplies at the wrapping table to prepare their gifts for their own trees at home. As kids work, pass around a poster board designed to look like a giant thank-you card. Have everyone sign the giant card and include appreciative comments for the parent volunteers.

Close the evening by going over to a group member's house to watch a classic Christmas movie such as *It's a Wonderful Life* or *A Christmas Carol*.

Hot News for Christmas!

This Christmas season have your kids create a newspaper that might have come out around the time of Jesus' birth. Include interviews with the shepherds and wise men; a news article titled "Census Wreaks Havoc" about early census returns; a scientific article titled "Unusual Star Seen," including quotes from the wise men; or an animal psychologist's views on the effects of the angels' visit on the sheep. With a little creativity and a photocopier, this could be a fun paper to pass out to the congregation.

Afterward lead the class through a discussion on "If the first Christmas happened today. . . " What things would be different? What would be the same? What would people say to an unmarried, pregnant teenager like Mary? How would our society react to angel visitations? Who would the wise men be in our society? Who would the Herod figure be? How would the slaughter of the children occur? Use *Matthew*

2:1-12 and *Luke 2:8-20* as the basis for this discussion.

Jesus Blankets for Christmas

A round Christmas time try this variation on traditional Christmas caroling. Collect basic art supplies that can be used on cloth, such as permanent colored markers, glitter, glue, scissors, colored felt panels, and puff paints. In addition bring sewing needles and heavy thread. Have kids each bring a plain blanket that their families no longer need. (Make sure blankets are in good condition.)

When everyone has arrived, explain that you want kids to transform their ordinary blankets into Jesus blankets using the supplies you've provided. Tell kids they can decorate their blankets in any way they wish. The only guideline is that the blankets must somehow illustrate Jesus or his qualities.

As kids finish, lay their blankets side by side and sew them loosely together to form one super-long Jesus blanket. Allow the blankets to dry overnight.

The next time your group meets, have kids gather at the church and take the Jesus blanket out for a night of caroling in a neighborhood near the church. Have kids huddle together in the blanket. Then have them shuffle from home to home singing Christmas carols to the residents.

At each home, have kids cut apart one of the individual blankets and give it to the residents. Continue until all the blankets have been given away.

LOW COST, NO COST
Food Ideas

Inexpensive ways to include food in
youth ministry.

That rumbling sound you hear isn't thunder rolling in the distance–it's your teenagers' stomachs growling in the youth group room. Try one of these mouthwatering, inexpensive food ideas to satisfy your youth group.

Blind Potluck

Tell group members you're going to share a "blind potluck" meal together at a particular young person's house. Tell kids to each bring anything that might be a useful part of a meal. For example, kids might bring leftovers (any kind), condiments, bread, tortillas, soft drinks, cheese, fruits, and so on.

Have kids bring their supplies to the designated young person's home. Gather all the supplies in the kitchen, then use *only* those supplies to plan and prepare a meal for the entire youth group to share. Once the meal is ready, have kids each take a plate full of whatever it is.

If the meal turns out well, consider writing down the recipes you came up with and sharing them with the congregation. If the meal turns out to be particularly awful, lead kids into the back yard and shout, "Food fight!" (Just kidding!)

Clean Your Pits

Have each person bring a fresh peach as admission to one of your youth group meetings (bring a few extras yourself in case some kids forget). Then have kids compete in a "clean your pits" race.

Make sure each group member has a fresh peach and a napkin. On "go," have kids race to eat their peaches, then clean their peach pits as thoroughly as possible. Tell kids they can use only their hands and mouth to clean the pit.

After two minutes, stop the race and inspect the peach pits. Find the person with the cleanest peach pit and declare him or her the winner.

After the race, use *1 John 1:8-9* as the basis for a discussion on how we can become clean in God's eyes.

Daniel Test

After a study of *Daniel 1*, ask your kids to take part in a Daniel test.

Form two groups. Ask one group to spend the next 10 days eating nothing but vegetables and water. Ask the other group to eat only rich foods, such as pizza, burgers, burritos, and other typical teenage food for the next 10 days. During the test period have members of both groups keep a brief daily journal of how they feel on all levels—physically, mentally, emotionally, and spiritually.

At the end of the 10 days, have members from both groups tell about their experience. Ask:

- **What do you think of Daniel's test now?**
- **What has this experience taught you about health? discipline? your relationship with God?**
- **Would you recommend that others take the Daniel test? Why or why not?**

Dependence Meal

Plan a sandwich lunch for your youth group. Designate specific groups of kids to bring the ingredients of the meal. For example, everyone whose last name begins with A-F might bring bread, everyone whose last name begins with G-L might bring lunch meat, and so on.

As kids arrive, have them form pairs. Once kids are seated next to their eating partners, explain that they're about to experience a "dependence meal." Tell kids that for the duration of the meal they're not allowed to feed themselves but they must feed each other. Tell kids this includes eating, drinking, and even wiping their chins.

When the meal is over, use *1 Corinthians 10:23-24* as the basis for a Bible study about interdependence within the body of Christ. Ask questions such as:

- **What's your first impression after this experience?**
- **How have people used our dependence meal as an opportunity for abuse? for caring?**
- **Why is being dependent on others so difficult?**
- **How can we build interdependence in our lives with other Christians?**

Food Search

Form groups of four to six and give each group a box of crackers (or something similar). Tell groups they have one hour to go into the neighborhood surrounding the church and try to "trade up" their crackers for a better snack. For example, a group might trade its crackers for two cans of peaches. Then at the next house, the group might trade its canned peaches for a loaf of bread and a soft drink. At the next house the group might trade its loaf of bread for sandwiches and more drinks. Have groups continue for the full hour or until they've got a meal they're satisfied with. Make sure groups identify themselves to residents and explain the goal of the activity.

When all the groups have returned, have each group show what it ended up with, then enjoy the meal together.

Note: It's usually best to send at least one adult volunteer with each group when you're sending kids door to door. If it seems unsafe to do this activity in the neighborhood around your church, have kids go only to your church members' homes.

Fruit Feast

Use this fun food idea next time you want to study *Romans 12:4-8* or *1 Corinthians 12:12-27*.

On a predetermined evening ask kids to come to the church for a fruit feast. Have kids each bring a different kind of fruit (the more variety the better). Purchase a watermelon and cut it in half using a jagged line (as in the diagram). Use a small scoop to

make melon balls as you empty out the inside of the watermelon. This will be your fruit bowl for the feast.

As kids arrive have them each cut up their fruit and place it in the feast bowl (the watermelon shell). Mix in each new fruit with the others to create a giant fruit salad. If possible, provide drinks, yogurt, or ice cream to go along with the feast.

While kids are eating have volunteers read aloud *Romans 12:4-8* or *1 Corinthians 12:12-27*. Ask:

- **How is the body of Christ like this fruit salad?**
- **How do we each add a different and unique flavor to Christ's body?**
- **What kind of fruit are you most like? Explain.**
- **What role do you often play in Christ's body?**
- **Why is that role important?**
- **How can we encourage each other in our unique roles in Christ's body?**

Miniature Food Meal

To feed a lot of people in a fun (and inexpensive) way, prepare miniature versions of their favorite foods. For example, one loaf of bread and a package of cocktail wieners can create a whole bunch of miniature hot dogs. Also, a package of chocolate frosting and a handful of Cheerios can be combined to make miniature chocolate doughnuts. For miniature pizza slices use triangle-shaped tortilla chips and drop a bit of pizza (or spaghetti) sauce and cheese on them before heating in the oven.

For added fun have kids sit at a miniature table (from a preschool room) and drink out of miniature cups during the meal.

While kids may not get filled up on these snacks, they certainly won't forget them.

Mixed-up Meal

Plan a spaghetti dinner for your youth group— along with garlic bread, corn, fruit salad, and pudding. Have kids earn each menu item by performing simple tasks for members of the congregation. Tell kids to work in groups of three to five as they're earning their food. For example, one group of teenagers might earn spaghetti noodles by running errands for a church member. Another group might earn garlic bread by babysitting choir members' children during choir practice.

At the dinner, have all the menu items numbered (except plates and drinks); for example, 1. forks, 2. spoons, 3. knives, 4. spaghetti, 5. corn, 6. garlic bread, 7. fruit salad, and 8. pudding.

Write each number that corresponds with a menu item on several small slips of paper and fold in half. Place all the folded papers in a basket. As kids arrive have them sit at tables set only with a plate and a drink. When everyone is seated, pass around the basket with the numbers in it. Have each person randomly choose eight pieces of paper.

Make a note of the number combinations each person chose and serve kids according to the numbers they picked. For example, if someone picked two eights give him or her two servings of pudding. Or if someone picks a four but not a one, he or she will have to find a creative way to eat the spaghetti. After all the kids are served, start the meal. Allow kids to trade or give away items if they wish.

The Most for Your Money

Meet on a Saturday morning for this event and have kids each bring a dollar as the price of admission. (You may want to have a few extra dollars handy in case some kids forget to bring money.)

Collect kids' money as they arrive. When everyone is ready, car pool to a nearby grocery store and meet in the parking lot. Form teams of no more than four and provide each team with $4 from the admission money.

Explain that teams will have 20 minutes to purchase as many *different* grocery items as possible for a youth group luncheon. Tell teenagers they can only use the money you provided to make their purchases. No additional funds may be added, and all groceries purchased must be donated to the luncheon.

Tell kids that no team can purchase more than one package of any given item, and remind them to consider the cost of the tax when deciding what to buy. Have kids save their receipts as proof of the amounts they spent.

When teams finish, collect all the items (and all the receipts). Applaud the team that got the most number of items and the team that got the most food by weight. After the contest take the group back to the church kitchen and have teenagers prepare and enjoy lunch using the supplies they bought.

 # Must-Eat Race

This is a great activity to do around harvest time in the fall. Have kids each bring one piece of fresh fruit or a vegetable as admission to one of your youth group meetings. Encourage group members to bring things like apples, pears, oranges, grapefruit, bell peppers, onions, broccoli, carrots, cucumbers, and grapes.

When everyone has arrived prepare two paper sacks full of assorted fresh fruits and vegetables. Make sure the two sacks have an equal assortment of items.

Form two lines, one facing the other. Tell kids they're going to participate in a food-eating relay race. Say: **I'll give one sack to the person at the front of each line. Those people must each pick something** out of the sack. They have only three seconds to grab something, so they'll have to do it quickly. Whatever each person grabs, he or she must eat it before passing the sack on to the next person in line. When the next person gets the sack, he or she will repeat the process, eating whatever comes out of the sack. We'll continue until the last person in line has finished eating whatever he or she pulls out of the sack.

Once you're sure everyone understands, start the race. No matter what kids pull out of the sack, don't allow them to trade or pass (unless they're allergic to the item). Also, make sure kids don't feel around in the sack for something they recognize. Just have them put their hand in and quickly pull out an item. Reward the winning team by distributing any left-over food among them.

Pizza Scavenger-Hunt

For this food event you'll provide the kitchen and the pizza crusts (have kids bring $1 to cover the cost), and kids will supply the rest.

Before the event, call members of your church congregation and let them know that you'll be sending kids out to collect particular pizza ingredients. Ask church members to participate by giving kids any food items they have available.

Form teams of four (each team gets one pizza crust). Tell teams they're responsible for topping their own pizza. Explain that team members can get the toppings only by going to church members' homes and asking for them. Team members must take whatever they're given. The only catch is that team members may not say or write any of the following words for the duration of the hunt:

- pizza
- topping
- crust
- food
- eat
- round
- pepperoni
- mushroom
- Canadian bacon
- cheese

Provide each team with an address list of church members and tell them they may go only to these houses. Give the teams 30 minutes to an hour to gather their items, depending on the size of your community.

When everyone returns, have teams build, bake, and eat their pizzas!

 # Potato Heads

Before this event have kids sign up to bring various toppings for potatoes; for example, sour cream, green onions, canned chili, cheese, mushrooms, steamed broccoli, margarine—basically anything kids think might be tasty. Buy a large bag of potatoes and have kids help wash them. Rub a small amount of vegetable oil on each potato. Then use a fork to poke holes in each potato and bake the potatoes at 350 degrees for 45 minutes to an hour, until done.

While the potatoes are baking, use the leftover potatoes to play "potato games" with the group. Here are a few games you can play:

Potato Baseball—Play this the same as regular baseball, except you use a potato for a ball (no power hitters allowed!).

Potato Roll—Kids roll potatoes toward a masking tape line on the floor. The potato that stops closest to the line without going past it wins.

Potato Sculptures—Kids carve faces in potatoes. The face that looks most like your senior pastor wins.

Potato Jugglers—Kids compete to see who can juggle the most potatoes at once. This is also fun when played in pairs.

When the potatoes in the oven are ready, set out the toppings and have kids serve themselves.

COST-CUTTING TIP

Cheap Eats—Serve popcorn often as a youth group treat. It's one of the cheapest snacks you'll find (you can buy it in bulk in some stores).

Refrigerator Raiders

Get parents' permission to raid their refrigerators for a fun youth group meal. Then cart kids around in groups of no more than six to visit group members' houses and find one item of food in each refrigerator that they can take back to the church to eat. Kids can only take one food item from each house, and the item must be approved by the group member's parent.

This activity can be especially fun when kids are collecting items for the other groups to eat!

To add a twist to this activity, announce a specific type of food to be collected (such as Italian food,

Mexican food, or pizza toppings) or have a "left-overs only" refrigerator raid.

Vegetable Cookout

Here's a healthy, low cost variation of the wee-nie roast. Ask church members to donate an assortment of vegetables for kids to roast, such as onions, green peppers, carrots, radishes, and broccoli.

Invite kids to a bonfire cookout and have them each bring their own meat—chicken, beef, or pork. When kids arrive have them cut their meat into small chunks. Give each person a shish kebab skewer to use for roasting. (Most discount stores carry these at an inexpensive price.) Have kids add the vegetables to their meat to create their own shish kebabs, then roast them on the open fire.

Of course, you can roast marshmallows for dessert.

COST-CUTTING TIP

Pizza Deal—While you can usually get a discount on pizzas when you buy more than four from a local pizza restaurant, nothing can beat the deal of buying cheap frozen pizzas and having kids bring extra toppings from home to spice them up.

LOW COST, NO COST
Outrageous Activities Using Everyday Stuff

Fun activities that use ordinary items
in surprising ways.

It's true that you can't make a mountain out of a molehill. But you *can* create unforgettable activities for your youth group using ordinary things like name tags, old tires, plastic soft drink bottles, and aluminum cans.

You don't believe it? Read on. If this section doesn't convince you, nothing will!

Affirmation Labels

As teenagers enter the room for your next youth group meeting, place a blank self-adhesive name tag on each person's back. When everyone is ready, have each person write one positive, descriptive word on each group member's name tag. Tell kids that no word can be used twice on the same name tag.

When everyone has finished, have teenagers form a circle on the floor. Have everyone remove their name tags and read what others have written about them. Then read aloud *1 Peter 1:22–2:1*. Encourage kids to train their hearts to see the good in others, not only the bad. Also encourage kids to reconcile with anyone in the youth group they have a problem with.

Tell group members to take their name tags home and stick them near their beds, on their mirrors, or even inside the covers of their Bibles to remind them of the good others see in them.

Bowling for Bodies

When teenagers' finances make a trip to the bowling alley impossible, try this innovative substitute.

In the church parking lot (or some other paved open area), set out one or two old tires. Form two equal teams—the Pinbrooks and the Pinfields. Have the Pinbrooks arrange themselves like bowling pins in an alley. However, tell the Pinbrooks to face several different directions *away* from the other team. Have the Pinfields grab the old tires and line up about 30 feet away.

One at a time, have the Pinfields take turns "bowling" a tire toward the Pinbrooks. Whoever the tire bumps into must take three steps in whatever direction he or she is facing. If that movement causes the "pin" to run into another pin, then that person must also take three steps in whatever direction he or she is facing—and so on. Every pin that moves is considered a downed pin and worth one point. Score spares and strikes according to normal bowling rules.

Play a full game, having teams take turns being the "pins" and the "bowlers." Tally the points at the end of the game and give the winning team a prize.

Note: Caution kids not to get too rough in the way they roll the tires or run into other pins.

Bowling for Bottles

Here's another alternative to visiting a bowling alley.

Ask church members or youth group parents to save plastic two-liter soft drink bottles so your group can have a bowling night. Collect enough bottles to create your own parking lot bowling alley with several bowling lanes.

Fill the plastic bottles with a few inches of sand or water to give them weight. In each bowling lane, set up 10 bottles in bowling-pin formation.

Form bowling teams and have teams bowl against each other by rolling basketballs or kickballs at the pins (the plastic bottles). Have members of each team take turns retrieving the balls and resetting the pins after each attempt. Make sure you have enough bowling lanes so all the teams can play at once.

Set up a double-elimination tournament in which winners play winners, and losers play losers. If a team loses twice, it's out of the tournament. Award the winning team with a gold-painted plastic soft drink bottle.

Canned Art Studios

After a day of collecting aluminum cans for recycling, have a mini-art festival with your youth group.

Form "artist studios" (groups of no more than five kids). Provide each studio with two or three trash bags full of aluminum cans, along with tape and glue. Have each studio produce its own work of art using only the cans and other supplies you've provided. If kids have trouble thinking up sculptures to create, suggest a castle, a rocket, or an animal.

Display kids' creations in the church foyer the following Sunday. A week or two later have kids disassemble the sculptures and take the cans to be recycled.

Drip Paintings

Form groups of no more than three. Seat groups at tables and give each trio a sheet of aluminum foil, a lighter, and a few old candles.

Tell groups they're each going to use the lighter and candles to make a drip painting—literally letting the melted wax drip down on the foil to create the painting. Explain that you'll assign each group an item to paint.

The items you assign can be anything from nature, as long as kids know what they are; for example, a lion, a butterfly, a tree, a person, and so on.

When the paintings are finished, have trios take turns showing and explaining their work (tell kids to leave their paintings on the foil). Then lead kids in a discussion comparing their drip paintings to God's awesome, creative work in nature. Use *Genesis 1* as the Bible basis for the discussion.

Afterward, hang the drip paintings on a wall of the youth room as a constant reminder of God's creative power.

Gelatin Hubcaps

At your next food event, use ordinary hubcaps as creative gelatin molds. Clean and disinfect the hubcap, then seal any openings with aluminum foil and tape. Then simply turn the hubcap upside down and pour in the prepared gelatin. Allow the gelatin to congeal in the refrigerator overnight. When food time comes, you're ready for a neat snack served in a uniquely creative way.

Other foods you can serve in hubcaps are salads, pudding, soup, dip, cookies, even pies (if you're very careful).

Guessing Beans

Use this mixer to help group members get to know each other. Secretly give kids each one to five beans and tell them to hide the beans in one hand.

Form pairs. Let kids each guess the number of beans in their partner's hand. If one or both of the partners guess incorrectly, have them find new partners. If they both guess correctly, have the pair sit down together on the floor and watch.

After several minutes, stop the activity and ask:

● **How did it feel to try to guess the number of beans in other people's hands? Explain.**

● **How is this activity—going around the group and trying to guess the number of beans each person holds—like trying to get to know people and make new friends?**

● **If beans were personality traits, what kinds of beans would you look for in a potential new friend?**

● **What can we learn from this activity to help members of our group get to know each other better?**

To close the activity, form a circle and have kids take turns tossing their beans into a bowl in the center. For each bean tossed, have the person tossing it tell one thing about himself or herself that others might not know. Kids might tell about things like their favorite hobbies, unusual places they've visited, the best movie they've ever seen, or favorite sports teams.

Nifty Newspapers

Here's an idea to help your teenagers understand the importance of trusting God with their lives.

At one of your regular meetings, provide an abundant supply of old newspapers, tape, and wire coat hangers. Using these supplies, have kids build their own paper fortresses. Encourage kids to use any design they wish. The only rule is that they must use only the supplies you've provided.

When kids finish, have them each show off their creations. Try to determine which fortress is the most sturdy. Then read together *Psalm 127*. Ask:

● **How do you feel about your fortress?**
● **How is building a fortress out of paper like trying to build your life without trusting God?**
● **What are ways we can keep ourselves from laboring in vain to build things in our lives?**

● In what ways are you still struggling to give God control over the blueprint of your life? What can you do about that?

Penny for Your Thoughts

This activity uses the smallest measure of money, a penny, to bring home the vastness of God's power.

Form five teams (a team can be one person). Give each team a roll of 50 pennies, a pencil, and paper. Assign each team one of the following questions to answer:

● **If 1 billion pennies were placed flat on the ground in a straight connected line, how long would the line be?**

● **How many gallon milk jugs would 1 billion pennies fill?**

● **How much would 1 billion pennies weigh?**

● **If 1 billion pennies were stacked one on top of each other, how tall would the stack be?**

● **How many football fields could be covered by 1 billion pennies laid flat, side by side?**

On a table in the room set out a ruler, a tablespoon measure (with a chart for converting tablespoons to cups, and cups to gallons), a scientific weight scale (borrow one from the local high school), an encyclopedia (Volume "F" for "football"), and several calculators.

Give each team paper and pencils and have them mathematically figure out the answers. (Don't tell kids that you don't know what the correct answers are until they've completed their calculations.) When the teams have all completed their assignments, have them each report their findings and how they arrived at them. Then have teams discuss these questions:

- **What's your reaction to the immenseness of 1 billion pennies?**
- **Did your results surprise you? Why or why not?**
- **Can you comprehend what 1 billion pennies looks like? Why or why not?**

Have groups read and summarize *Psalm 139:1-18.* Ask:

- **How does it affect you to hear about the vast power of God?**
- **What does this passage tell you about God's love for you?**
- **How can knowing this truth change the way you live?**

Rubber Band Head

Here's a wacky game for kids having a bad-hair day.

Form groups of three and give each group a bag of hair rubber bands. Have each group choose one person to be a model. Tell the groups you're going to have a contest to see which group can make the most unusual hairstyle out of their model using only the hair bands.

For example, kids might create a unicorn look with a ponytail on the front of a model's head, or they might string several hair bands together to drape over a model's ears. Encourage groups to be creative and have fun.

Allow four minutes, then judge each hairstyle. Award 1 point for every hair band used and give a general score of 1 to 10 (10 being best) for overall weirdness of hair.

Have teams choose new models and repeat the process for as long as time allows. Tell teams they'll be disqualified for duplicating what others have already done or for copying any other team's work.

After all rounds, tally each team's points. Give the team with the highest overall score a bag of hair rubber bands to share.

 # Scars

Give each person a 3×5 card and a pen. Have kids write on their cards "hurts" they've experienced that have significantly affected them; for example, the death of a loved one, a failed relationship, an abusive relationship, hurt from parents, rejection by others, or a major failure. Make sure kids understand that no one will see their lists.

Once the lists are finished, give kids each a charcoal briquette. Have kids place a charcoal "scar," a long mark on their faces, for every item on their lists (if kids are unwilling to mark their faces, have them mark their arms). When everyone is "scarred," ask:

● **How does going through a hurtful time leave scars on a person?**

● **How do you feel knowing that other people can see your charcoal scars?**

● **How do scars from our past affect what we do today?**

● **Is it ever good to go through a scarring experience in life? Explain your answer.**

● **How can we find healing for the scars left over from our past?**

Form pairs and give each person a damp cloth. Have partners silently clean each other's faces (or arms) while you read aloud *Isaiah 53:1-5* to close.

Sin Washings

Give each person a bar of soap, a butter knife, a spoon, and a fork. (Check with a local hotel or motel to see if they'll donate their leftover soap for you to use.) Ask kids to carve their bars of soap into a statue or symbol that represents God's forgiveness.

When kids finish, have them form groups of no more than four and explain their carvings to their group members. Then have each person in the foursomes read one of these Scriptures to his or her group: *Psalm 51:7-9*; *1 Corinthians 6:9-11*; *Titus 3:3-6*; and *1 John 1:9*.

Afterward, have groups discuss these questions:
- **How is God's forgiveness like or unlike soap?**
- **Why does the Bible use the analogy of being washed when it talks about forgiveness?**
- **How does it feel to be forgiven? to forgive?**

Have kids each take their soap carvings home and use them the next time they shower. Ask kids to confess their sins as they're bathing and receive God's forgiveness in their lives.

Soft Drink Heaven

Sponsor a soft drink heaven theme night for your youth group. In the weeks before the event, collect several bags of empty and uncrushed soft drink cans to use for games. Ask for donations from your teenagers, church members, friends and neighbors.

At the event, try these activities:
- **Have kids come dressed in their favorite soft drink paraphernalia.** Kids can wear shirts, hats,

buttons, or anything else that advertises a particular brand of soft drink.

- **Play Base Can.** Play by normal baseball rules but substitute a broom for a bat and empty soft drink cans for balls.

- **Make soft drink castles.** Form teams of no more than four and give each team a bag of soft drink cans. Have kids compete to build the most elaborate castle using only the cans. Set a five-minute time limit.

- **Play Seek and Crush.** Before the meeting, make several piles of uncrushed cans according to brand; for example, all Coke cans in one pile, all Pepsi cans in another, and so on. Make sure you have an equal number of cans in each pile, then hide all the cans on church grounds.

At the meeting, form as many teams as there are piles and assign each team one of the brands. Set a time limit and send the teens out to search for the hidden cans. If kids find another team's brand of can, they must crush it and leave it hidden for that team to find.

At the appointed time, have teams return to the room to compare results. Award 10 points for each crushed can brought back and 25 points for each uncrushed can brought back. The team with the most points wins.

 # Strings of Stress

Form a circle. Pass around a ball of string and a pair of scissors. Have kids each name all the stresses in their life. Stresses can be anything from grades to parents to a recent fight with their best friend. For each stress they name, have kids each pull out one foot of string. Once they've named all the stresses they can think of, have kids each cut their string off the ball.

Once everyone has shared and has a length of string, form trios. Have kids tie up each of their trio partners using that person's string. Encourage kids to make their group members as immobile as possible without hurting anyone (you'll have to help tie the last person in each trio).

Once everyone is tied up, lead the group in a mini-aerobics routine. Turn on some music and take kids through a sequence of marching in place, jumping jacks, side hops, and other exercises.

Stop the music. While kids are still tied up, ask:
- **How do you feel being all tied up?**
- **How is the effect of this string similar to the effect of stress in your life?**
- **How does stress rob your sense of freedom?**
- **Is it possible to live so that stress doesn't have this effect on you? Why or why not?**

Read aloud *Philippians 4:6-7.* Ask:
- **Is it possible to not be stressed about anything, as this passage suggests? Why or why not?**
- **According to this passage, what's the best way to deal with stress? Why is that hard to do?**
- **How can we help each other reduce the stress in our lives?**

Have kids work to set each other free from the string. Then, with the string heaped in a pile in the middle of each trio, have kids pray together for God to show them ways to be stress reducers for each other this week.

Summer Sledding

When summer gets so hot it makes you wish for snow, tell kids to bring large cardboard squares and have a summer sledding party.

Have kids rub one side of their cardboard section with paraffin wax. Make sure the wax completely covers the entire length of the cardboard.

Take the group to a large grassy hill and start sledding. Hold contests for fastest sled, slowest sled, most people on a single sled, most people standing on a sled in motion, most artistic expression while sledding, and so on.

After everyone is worn out from sledding, top off the event by traveling to a convenience store for a super-cold, super-huge drink.

Toilet Paper Roll Slingshots

Have kids create these unique slingshots to use in a game of Paper-Wad Tag.

Give kids each one empty toilet paper roll and a rubber band. At one end of their rolls have kids punch two holes, one directly across from the other. Cut the rubber band to make one piece. Tie each end through one of the holes.

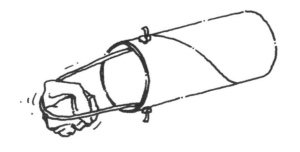

Demonstrate how to use the slingshot by putting a small paper wad into the rubber band sling and shooting it through the barrel formed by the toilet paper roll.

Next, form two teams and play several rounds of Paper-Wad Tag. In the game, opposing team members shoot each other with paper wads using the slingshots. Every person who's hit with a paper wad is out of the game. The last person remaining wins the game for his or her team.

For a milder variation of this game, set up extra toilet paper rolls as targets and have kids compete to knock over the most targets per shot.

Uncommon Commercials

Form four teams. Give each team a common item, such as a bag of rubber bands, or a box of paper clips, toothpicks, or pencils—anything you have in your home or office. Give teams 10 minutes to develop a commercial for their object. However, tell groups they can't advertise the object's conventional use. Instead, they must create a new use for the product and advertise the item in this new way.

For example, a group could connect paper clips into a large chain and advertise it as versatile jewelry (necklace, bracelet, and earrings all in one).

When everyone is ready, have a dueling-commercials time where kids try to outdo each other in the way they present their commercials. Award small prizes for the most unusual commercial, best overall commercial, and funniest commercial.

Who's Got the Goods?

Use this game to help kids explore their attitudes toward money.

Give each person a different number of sunflower seeds and announce that sunflower seeds have become the currency of the day. Explain that on "go," kids can give seeds to anyone they wish, take seeds from anyone they wish, or take seeds from one person and give them to another. Encourage rivalries by pointing out who has the most or fewest seeds at any given time.

After three minutes, stop the game and ask:

● **What did you think about the distribution of seeds?**

● **How would you describe your attitude during this game?**

● **How did our attitudes during the game compare to our attitudes about money?**

Form pairs. Have the oldest person in each pair read *1 Timothy 6:6-11*, and the youngest summarize it in one sentence. Then have pairs discuss these questions:

● **What's your reaction to this passage?**

● **Based on this passage, how would you describe a healthy attitude toward money?**

● **What can we learn from our game and this passage to help us maintain a healthy attitude about money?**

Have kids each put a sunflower seed in their purse, wallet, or pocket to keep as a reminder of what they learned during this activity.

LOW COST, NO COST

Fund-Raisers

Quick ways to raise money without
having to invest a mint.

No book of low cost, no cost ideas for youth ministry would be complete without at least one section of fund-raisers to supplement your youth budget. Try one of the ideas in this section the next time your group needs just a few dollars more.

Blessing Banners

Set up a "blessing banner" service through your church. For $5 or $10, individuals can buy a blessing banner with either a Scripture quote or personal message on it. Have kids set up a booth in the church foyer to take orders each Sunday, then deliver the banners to the appropriate people the following Sunday afternoon.

To make each banner, gather a roll of newsprint (or several sheets of poster board), lots of 2–foot sticks (to use as stakes), markers, glue, glitter, and thumbtacks. Have kids write on the newsprint (or poster board) whatever the person wants to say, then decorate it to create a colorful banner. Allow kids to use the supplies you've gathered. Have kids with artistic ability draw on the banner. Have others get a book of calligraphy and

COST-COMMUNICATION TIP

Budget Communication—Encourage a team spirit toward money problems. Be honest as you discuss youth group expenses. Remember that we're preparing kids to live on their own, and finances will be a major future concern. And, of course, don't allow ridicule of any kind toward kids who have financial problems. It takes only a comment or two to damage a young person's self-esteem in this area.

trace or copy fancy letters for the words.

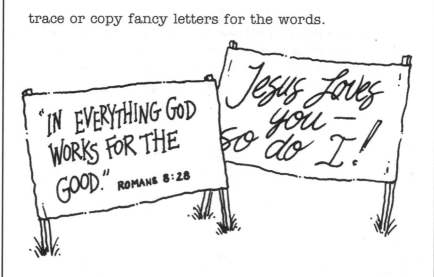

The next Sunday have kids deliver each banner to the appropriate home by tacking the banner to two wooden stakes, then driving the stakes into the person's front yard. Have kids ring the doorbell, then run away.

 # Buy-a-Square

Is it time to paint your youth group room? If so, turn the event into a fun (and colorful) fund-raiser. First you'll need to collect a variety of wall paint from church members and local decorating stores. See how many different colors can be donated.

Next have kids section off the walls in the youth room into 2-foot squares using a yardstick and a pencil.

Prepare a corresponding map that diagrams how the room has been sectioned off and make photocopies of the map for kids to use. Include a list of the color options for the sections shown on the map.

Assign different portions of the room to each group member and give each person a copy of the map. Then have kids go out and find sponsors from the congregation willing to contribute a dollar or more to "buy" a section of the wall. People who buy the squares get to choose the paint colors for those squares.

When all the squares have been purchased, kids can begin painting. After all the squares have been painted, display a version of the map (with all the colors filled in) to the congregation. Include a list of all the people who bought squares along with a note of thanks to them.

Church Milk-Carton Boat Race

If you have access to a river or stream, you can start a yearly tradition in your congregation with this fun spring fund-raising idea.

About five weeks before the event, invite kids and adults to form joint teams of no more than four for an all-church milk-carton boat race. Have each team pay an entry fee of $5.

For teams to enter the race, they must each create a riverboat using only cardboard milk cartons, duct tape, and oil-based markers or paint. Explain that awards will be given not only for the fastest boat, but also for the largest, the tallest, the most unusual, and the most artistic.

Over the next several weeks, advertise the boat race as a fun event for the whole family. Sell tickets to the race for $1 each, explaining how the money will be spent. Tell families to "BYOP"—bring your own picnic—to the event.

A few days before the race, go to a nearby river

or stream and use flags to mark out a 300-yard course. Assign volunteers to act as judges for all the categories. Prepare award certificates to be presented to each member of the winning teams.

On the day of the race, have families come early for a picnic. At race time have people line up along the shore to watch the action (be sure to reserve a special area for the judges). Set up portable stereos to provide racing music, then start the race.

After the race have the judges award the various certificates to the winning teams. Repeat the event each year—both for fun and as an effective fund-raiser.

Cupid's Helper

As Valentine's Day approaches, tell your church members that the youth group will be offering a Valentine's Day delivery service. Charge customers according to the amount of work you will have to do.

For example, charge around $5 for simple delivery of an item provided by the person—a teddy bear, flowers, candy, or balloons. Charge $7 to deliver the item and recite a message from the sender. Offer singing telegrams for $10. Make sure you have enough students, cars, and time to make all the deliveries on Valentine's Day.

Day of Silence

Plan a special day of silence for the members of your youth group. Several weeks beforehand, have kids find sponsors willing to donate a certain dollar amount for each hour kids remain silent.

On the day of the event, have kids meet at the church to begin their time of silence. Then take kids out for a day of interesting events that require them to interact with other people. Let them experience what it's like to live without the ability to speak. Go to the mall, go out to eat in a restaurant, play a game of volleyball, or go to a museum.

At the end of the day, give the kids each a scoop of ice cream and have them yell, "I scream, you scream, we all scream for ice cream!" Have kids discuss what their day was like and what they learned from the experience.

The next week have kids collect the money from their sponsors.

Flower Delivery

Contact area florists to find out if they need additional help delivering flowers on their busiest days of the year. Offer the services of your group members to work for florists by delivering flowers on those days. (Make sure the kids have drivers' licenses and good driving records.) Most florists do extra business on Mother's Day, Father's Day, and Valentine's Day and are glad to pay for the extra help.

Lawn Mower Marathon

During the summer offer to mow lawns for people in your church. Advertise that your group members will be dedicating one day to lawn mowing, and have interested customers sign up for the service. Charge between $5 and $10 per lawn.

Make sure you have enough teenagers and equipment to mow all the lawns in the time you promised (each person can probably mow three or four lawns in one day).

To make the project go more smoothly, assign customers to teams of kids according to location. Arrange for your adult leaders to transport kids from house to house and make sure they have enough gas for the day's work. It's usually best to have kids mow in teams of two or three, if possible.

The day of the fund-raiser, have someone at church stay near a phone so teams can call in their progress and be dispatched to areas that still need to be covered. At each job have kids leave an evaluation form on the front door so owners can check the work. If for any reason a customer is dissatisfied, have teams return to that home and correct the problem to the owner's satisfaction.

COST-CUTTING TIP

Low-Fee Retreat—To reduce the dollars kids need to pay for a youth group retreat, have a "bring your own food" retreat. Ask parents to work with kids to prepare the food they'll need for the retreat. Then meet before your departure to pack the food in coolers.

Money in the Bag

Set aside a Saturday for kids to travel all around your city picking up trash. Before the event have adults in your congregation sign up to pay a certain amount for every bag of trash the group collects.

If your group is large enough, split into teams and go to different parts of the city where trash may be more abundant, such as major highways, parks, and other public places. At the end of the day, gather all the bags back at the church. Then, on Sunday, have kids collect pledges from adults.

My Fair Share

For this fund-raising idea, you'll need photocopies of the one-share stock coupon (p.138) that you can distribute to church members.

Explain to group members that they'll be selling these coupons as individual "shares" in youth ministry services. All money collected from the shares can be used for upcoming youth events. Each share (coupon) costs $1, and a person may purchase as many as he or she wants.

In the foyer of the church, create a chart that details how many shares are required for each service teenagers will render to shareholders. Possible services include:

- grass cutting—seven shares
- car wash—five shares
- baby-sitting—two to three shares per hour
- garage cleaning—10 shares
- dog walking—one share per dog

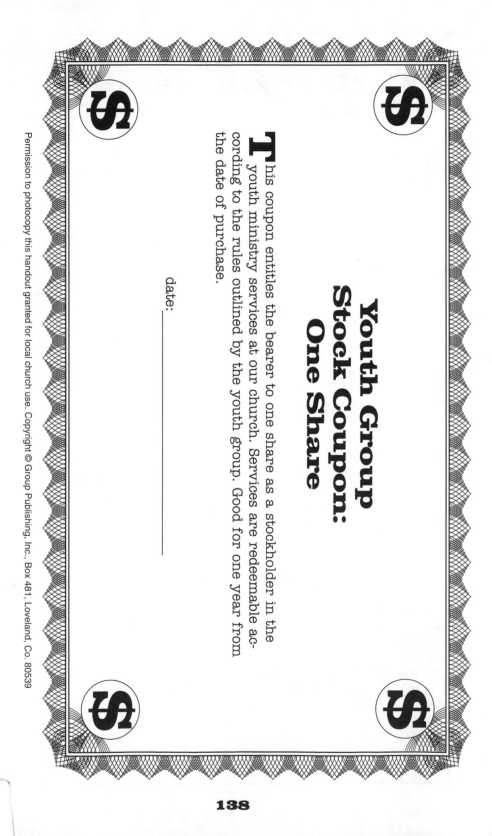

Youth Group
Stock Coupon:
One Share

This coupon entitles the bearer to one share as a stockholder in the youth ministry services at our church. Services are redeemable according to the rules outlined by the youth group. Good for one year from the date of purchase.

date: _____

• pet washing—two shares per pet
• grocery shopping—three shares
• leaf raking—seven shares
• gutter cleaning—five shares

Use your imagination to come up with other uses for shares. Shares may be used all at once or saved for future events but must be used within one year from the date of purchase.

Pack the House

Contract with one of the popular eating establishments in your area for a "pack-the-house" night or weekend. During the prescribed time the restaurant donates an agreed-upon percentage of each person's bill to the church or another charity organization—if that person identifies himself or herself with the pack-the-house event.

Advertise the event through your church publications. Have kids encourage neighbors, friends, and relatives to support the pack-the-house event. This is a great way to raise funds while building community awareness.

Research Teams

Have kids form research teams of no more than four kids each. These teams will raise money by researching information or finding specific items for members of the congregation.

Have people pay a nominal research fee to hire a team to uncover whatever information or objects they want the team to find. Teams might be hired to look for anything from the birthday of a famous actor to an old record once loved but long lost.

Then have teams look around town for the item(s) and collect them (or explain where they can be found if not free) for the person who hired them. If kids find the actual item within a specified time limit (two days or so), they also could receive a finder's fee from the person who hired them.

This activity can continue year-round. Spring and summer are often the best times for these activities as garage and yard sales provide all kinds of opportunities to find things.

People who hire the research teams may also have the option of providing kids with a few dollars to purchase a specific item if it is found.

COST-CUTTING TIP

Hour Power—To help kids earn money for a concert or other special event, reward them for participating in your fund-raisers.

Keep a logbook of the hours each person works at a fund-raiser. Count the total amount of money raised (minus expenses). Divide it by the total number of hours worked by all the kids. Then credit each young person's "concert account" this amount multiplied by the number of hours he or she worked.

Be sure that group members who worked all day will have enough credits to pay for a ticket. Otherwise you'll need another fund-raiser. Tell the kids that if their credits exceed the ticket price, the extra money will remain in the general youth group fund.

These Shoes are Made for Servin'

Here's a unique fund-raising idea for the next time your group goes on a mission trip.

Have kids each loan you a pair of their shoes (label each pair so you don't forget which shoes go with which feet). Set up a banner in the church foyer describing the nature and cost of your mission trip. Assign each shoe an equal dollar value (such as $100) and line up the shoes side by side on the floor. Ask church members to donate money for the mission trip by placing their donations in the shoes.

Once a shoe has collected its assigned amount of money, remove it from the line up. Continue to encourage donations each week until all the shoes are removed.

Valet Parking

Expensive restaurants do it, so why not your youth group? Dress up your older group members and provide a valet parking service for church attendees on a Sunday morning.

Have group members keep track of the keys, car locations, and the names of the owners. Let the church members know in advance that you'll be providing this service for them (if they desire it)—and inform them that tips will be greatly appreciated!

Innovative Resources For Your Ministry...

The Practical Youth Ministry Handbook

Here's the perfect resource for youth workers looking for practical ideas that will really work. These are tested ideas that have improved youth ministries all across the country. First, you'll discover practical articles packed with valuable information on topics such as...
- assessing teenagers' needs,
- recruiting and training volunteers,
- working with parents, and
- understanding group dynamics.

Part two gives actual meeting plans that will make Bible learning fun and unforgettable for your teenagers. You'll save loads of time by choosing from...
- community builders,
- fund-raisers,
- fun learning games,
- quick devotions, and
- outreach and service projects.

This valuable new book will give you the practical tools missing from many seminary and Bible college youth ministry curricula.

ISBN 1-55945-175-0

Pick & Choose: Program Ideas for Youth Ministry

Use these 200 creative ideas for customizing your meetings. Simply pick the program elements you need—and presto—your programming is done! Choose from winning...
- Crowdbreakers and Games,
- Outreach and Service Projects,
- Group Builders and Affirmations,
- Holiday and Seasonal Activities,
- Quick Devotions,
- Worship Ideas,
- On-Location Meeting Ideas,
- Active Discussion Starters.

And **Pick & Choose** is so easy to use. Decide what elements you need from the sections listed on the front of the box. Flip through the section you need and find the resource card you want for your meeting. Or choose more than one and create an entirely new meeting.

Each card lists a title or theme, appropriate group size, activity length, and needed supplies. For handy reference, each card has space to list when you've used the idea—so you don't repeat an idea more often than you want.

Become a programming whiz with **Pick & Choose**!

ISBN 1-55945-199-8

Order today from your local Christian bookstore, or write: Group Publishing, Box 485, Loveland, CO 80539. For mail orders, please add postage/handling of $4 for orders up to $15, $5 for orders of $15.01+. Colorado residents add 3% sales tax.

Devotional Resources For Your Ministry...

Devotions for Youth Groups

Get 52 quick devotions in each book that need little or no preparation—on important topics such as...
- love,
- friendship,
- rumors,
- peer pressure,
- faith,
- accepting others,
- grades,
- peace,
- service,

...and more. Each is complete with Scripture reference, attention-grabbing learning experience, discussion questions, and closing. Bring teenagers closer to God with these refreshing devotions!

10-Minute Devotions for Youth Groups
J.B. Collingsworth
ISBN 0-931529-85-9

More 10-Minute Devotions for Youth Groups
ISBN 1-55945-068-1

10-Minute Devotions for Youth Groups, Volume III
ISBN 1-55945-171-8

Devotions for Youth Groups On the Go

Dan and Cindy Hansen

Now it's easy to turn every youth group trip into an opportunity for spiritual growth for your kids. This first-of-its-kind resource gives you 52 easy-to-prepare devotions that teach meaningful spiritual lessons using the experiences of your group's favorite outings. You'll get devotions perfect for everything from amusement parks...to choir trips...to miniature golf...to the zoo. Your kids will gain new insights from the Bible as they...
- discuss how many "strikes" God gives us...after enjoying a game of softball,
- experience the hardship of Jesus' temptation in the wilderness...on a camping trip,
- understand the disciples' relief when Jesus calmed the storm...while white-water rafting, even
...learn to trust God's will when bad weather cancels an event or the bus breaks down!

Plus, the handy topical index makes your planning easy.
ISBN 1-55945-075-4

More Creative Resources From *Group*®...

Ready-to-Go Meetings for Youth Ministry

Save yourself time and energy—planning meetings your teenagers will love. Each of the 70 meetings includes clear instructions and carefully constructed discussion questions to make planning simple. All you have to do is collect the supplies and go!

Meetings explore issues facing teenagers today in fun, creative ways. Topics include...

- coping with fear,
- forgiveness,
- gossip,
- appearances,
- dating,
- friendship,
- appreciating parents,
- learning to listen,
- drugs

...and dozens more that impact kids' lives.

With **Ready-to-Go Meetings for Youth Ministry**, your preparation is quick and easy. And your teenagers don't just hear the truth—they experience it! ISBN 1-55945-168-8

Controversial Discussion Starters for Youth Ministry

Stephen Parolini

Now it's easy to lead your teenagers in finding biblical answers to today's tough issues like abortion, euthanasia, and New Age philosophy...plus, important practical-living issues, such as cheating in school and lying to parents. Each issue is presented with two opposing position statements and supporting Scriptures. Teenagers then form debate groups and have the opportunity to argue the right and wrong of each issue. As kids talk and check the Bible, they begin to form convictions that will stay with them for a lifetime. ISBN 1-55945-156-4

Order today from your local Christian bookstore, or write: Group Publishing, Box 485, Loveland, CO 80539. For mail orders, please add postage/handling of $4 for orders up to $15, $5 for orders of $15.01+. Colorado residents add 3% sales tax.